A WALK IN FAITH

A WALK IN FAITH

A PERSONAL RECORD OF A FAITH WALK

KENNETH L. CANION

WESTBOW
P R E S S
A DIVISION OF THOMAS NELSON

ISBN: 978-1-4497-5490-7 (sc)

Library of Congress Control Number: 2012909857

WestBow Press books may be ordered through booksellers or by contacting:

WestBow Press
A Division of Thomas Nelson
1663 Liberty Drive
Bloomington, IN 47403
www.westbowpress.com
1-(866) 928-1240

Printed in the United States of America

WestBow Press rev. date: 06/19/2012

Preface

"A Walk in Faith" is written with a purpose in mind. It is designed to be used as a record of those truths revealed to me from day to day as a result of being in God's word and availing myself to prayer and having a quiet time with Him. I read His word and find it compelling. But reading is not enough. I find I must apply His Word to my life daily. So, by rising up early in the morning while my mind is fresh and before it is polluted by my daily struggle, I can record the principle truths or incidents that point to the integrity of His word in me.

So, the truths and events recorded here are those things I see in my life from day to day as illuminated in the glow of His Word. I do not know what I will write until I examine the previous daily activity in the dawn of each morning. These are impressions, thoughts, or reflections that indicate the good things that have been provided for me on a daily basis by the presence of the Holy Spirit. These recordings are the way I see my day as I look back and try to recount the wonderful provisions, lessons or truths given me. They are written from the experience first, and then scripture is applied.

The bias in my writing is from my belief in the Judeo-Christian God, Yahweh or Jehovah and His unprecedented visitation in the person of Jesus, the Christ, among humans living on earth. I believe He is the Gospel, the Good News, The Living Word and is as powerful and active today in the hearts of believers as when He was physically among us as a man. He is all man and all God simultaneously, existing today in the same form as He assumed during His earthly visit. He was born of a virgin, crucified and resurrected for the salvation of mankind, and dwells in us today in the person of the Holy Spirit.

Therefore, you are invited to take a three month journey with me in daily installments of His presence. Space is provided for your input, to yourself, on what the Holy Spirit may have revealed to you as a result of reading the Word of God in a slightly different approach.

DAY 1

The Lord is great, all the time. It is the little things that count. He is so faithful to reward me daily with His abundance.

It is such a simple task to fix breakfast. I open the pantry, food is there. I open the refrigerator, food is there. I turn the stove on, power is there. There is no shortage of daily sustenance blessing in my house.

How does all this come about? Is it by my own brilliance that we are so well provided for? Not! Did I choose my parents, my genetic makeup, my country, or even the age in which I was born?

I appreciate God's faithfulness in my daily provisions. I do not take anything for granted. The Lord is sovereign. He chose me; I wasn't even looking for Him. He called my name before I was born. He chose my perfect mate.

My choices are there too. I choose when to work, study, goof off, take things seriously or waste time. I am where I am because of the choices I have made. I cannot blame God for that.

God called me to choose Him. I chose Him. He rewards me every day of my life.

Bible Reference; Notes

1. God's goodness;

    <u>Deut. 30:9</u> – "…the Lord thy God will make you successful in everything you do…"

    <u>Jer. 29:11</u> – "For I know the plans I have for you… They are plans for good and not disaster, to give you a future and a hope."

    <u>Matt. 7:11</u> - "If you sinful people know how to give good gifts to your children, how much more will your Heavenly Father give good gifts to those who ask Him.?

2. God's provision;

    <u>PS 68:19</u> – "Praise the Lord, Praise God our savior, for each day He carries us in His arms."

    <u>PS 107:8</u> –"Let them praise the Lord for his great love and for all his wonderful deeds to them. For he satisfies the thirsty and fills the hungry with good things."

    <u>Rom. 13:14</u> –"But put on the Lord Jesus Christ and make no provision for the flesh in regard to its lusts."

3. My responsibility;

    <u>Josh. 24:15</u> –"But if you are willing to serve the Lord, then choose for yourselves this day whom you will serve…But as for me and my house, we will serve the Lord."

    <u>Ecc. 12:13</u> – Solomon's words –"Here is my final conclusion; Fear God, obey his commandments, for this is the duty (responsibility) of every person."

    <u>Luke 4:8</u> – Jesus' words –"The Scriptures say, 'You must worship the Lord your God, serve only him.'"

___

___

_____

_____

_____

_____

DAY 2

God is good, all the time. I awoke. I realized that I crawled out of a warm comfortable bed. My sweetie was lying next to me. It was peaceful; I had no worries. The Peace of God overwhelmed me. I had my quiet time. I was free to read, free to pray. I had a sense of peace from God. The Holy Spirit comforted me, communed with me in prayer.

My vehicle worked, it was comfortable; I was able to hear Christian singing on the CD player. I had a job to go to, received just compensation for my efforts and had money to spend.

A woman in the parking lot asked me for some gas money. My wallet was empty, but I was able to draw excess money from my bank card. She was grateful for the gift card for gasoline. I was thankful I could contribute to someone in need. God blessed us both.

I was welcomed home by my mate, the wife of my youth. We had food to eat, a bed to sleep in and a roof over our heads. I slept! Thank you Lord!

Bible Reference; Notes

1. God's Peace;

    <u>Lev. 26:6</u> – "And I will give peace in the land, and you shall lie down, and none shall make you afraid…"

    <u>Rom. 5:1</u> –"…since we have been made right in God's sight by faith, we have peace because of what Jesus Christ our Lord has done for us."

    <u>Phil. 4:7</u> – "…His peace will guard your hearts and minds as you live in Christ Jesus."

2. God's Blessing;

    <u>Deu. 11:27</u> – "You will be blessed if you obey the commandments of the Lord…"

    <u>Matt. 11:6</u> – "… God blesses those who are not offended by Him."

    <u>John 20:29</u> – "…Blessed are those who haven't seen me and believe anyway."

3. The Holy Spirit;

    <u>Mark 1:8</u> – John's words –"I baptize you with water, but he (Jesus) will baptize you with the Holy Spirit."

    <u>Luke 3:22</u> – "As he (Jesus) was praying, the heavens opened and the Holy Spirit descended on him in the form of a dove. And a voice from heaven said 'You are my beloved Son and I am fully pleased with you."

    <u>Romans 8:15, 16</u> – "…You should behave instead like God's very own children…For His Holy Spirit speaks to us deep in our hearts and tells us that we are God's children."

_____

_____

_____

_____

DAY 3

The Lord sustains me. He rescued my soul from torment today. I got up with the funk. All morning long I was being spiritually depressed I felt darkness had enveloped me. My mind had run afoul. It was full of dark thoughts and despair. I thought I was losing it. My thoughts were out of control!

All I could do was pray the names of God: Yahweh, Jehovah, El Shaddai, El Elohim, Jehovah-Jirah, Jehovah-shalom, Jehovah-Nissi, Jehovah-Tsediku, Jehovah-Shamma, Jehovah-Rapha, Adnoai, Aba, Father, King of Kings, Lord of Lords, Prince of Peace, Everlasting Father, Alpha & Omega, Beginning and Ending, King of the order of Melchizedek, Lion of the Tribe of Judah, Rock of Ages, Lover of my soul, Creator, Holy Spirit, Jesus, God.

The pale lifted from me! I am sane; God heard my cry and my mind has been restored!

Bible Reference; Notes

1. God's supply;

    2 Sam. 22:3 –"The Lord is my rock, my fortress, my savior; My God is my rock in whom I find protection. He is my shield, the strength of my salvation and my stronghold."

    Phil. 4:19 – "And this same God who takes care of me will supply all your needs from His glorious riches, which have been given to us in Christ Jesus."

2. God's Name;

    PS 34:3 –"Come let us tell of the Lord's greatness; let us exalt His name together."

    Matt. 12:21 – "And His name will be the hope of the entire world."

    Acts 2:21 – "And anyone who calls on the name of the Lord will be saved."

    Acts 4:12 – "There is salvation in no one else! There is no other name in all of heaven for people to call on to save them."

    Phil. 2:10 – "…so at the name of Jesus every knee will bow, in heaven and on earth and under the earth…"

3. God's blessing;

    Num. 6:24-26 –"May the Lord bless you and protect you. May the Lord smile on you and be gracious to you. May the Lord show you His favor and give you His peace."

    PS 34:8 –"O taste and see that the Lord is good; How blessed is the man who takes refuge in Him."

_____

_____

_____

_____

DAY 4

I had a good quiet time this morning, Lord. Days seem to run into each other. Sometimes I take for granted all the wonderful things in my life. I hope not ever to do that again, not too often anyway.

I have such freedom in the little, insignificant parts of life. For instance; Saturday, for us, is hotcake breakfast day. It is very simple, just open the pantry, find the ingredients and mix up the recipe. Run out of flour? Just buy some at the store. Need more bacon or sausage? Just buy some more.

God's blessings in this are; a store to go to, food available on the shelf, money available in the bank, an auto available in the drive, a stove, a house, knowledge, job for income, regular check coming in, civil rest, no revolution, looting gangs, freedom to move, no fear to travel. The list goes on and on.

In this country we are not prosperous because we are individually in control. We are prosperous because our Nation was built on a covenant relationship with God. We are receiving the blessings brought about by the Founding Fathers of the United States.

In our new course of national direction are we just about to give up on that covenant relationship with God? Father, I thank you for your past blessings and pray that we stay the course as One Nation under God.

Bible Reference; Notes

1. Still;

    PS 46:10 –"Be silent (still) and know that I am God. I will be honored by every nation. I will be honored throughout the world."

    2 Chron. 20:17 –"(The battle is not yours, but God's) –"But you will not even need to fight. Take your positions, then stand still and watch the Lord's victory. He is with you."

    1 Peter 3:4 –"You should be known for the beauty that comes from within, the unfading beauty of a gentle and quiet spirit which is precious to God."

2. Supply;

    2 Cor. 9:11 – (On giving) –"you will be enriched so you can give (supply others) even more generously."

    Phil. 4:19 –"And this same God who takes care of me will supply all your needs from his glorious riches, which have been given to us in Christ Jesus."

    1 Thes. 5:14 –"Brothers and sisters, we urge you to warn those who are lazy. Encourage those who are timid. Take tender care (supply) of those who are weak. Be patient with everyone."

3. Promise;

    Gal. 3:22 –"But the scriptures have declared that we are all prisoners of sin, so the only way to receive God's promise is to believe in Jesus Christ."

    Eph. 1:13 –"And now you also have heard the truth, the Good News that God saves you. And when you believed in Christ he identified you as his own by giving you his Holy Spirit whom he promised long ago."

<u>2 Peter 3:9</u> – "The Lord isn't really being slow about his promise to return, as some people think. No, he is being patient for your sake. He does not want anyone to perish so he is giving more time for everyone to repent."

_____

_____

_____

_____

_____

_____

DAY 5

Your miracle this day, Father, was great. This is Sunday. My wife and I freely and without resistance dressed and drove to church to worship you, the Lord God Almighty. No one stopped us; no one interfered with our freedom to worship.

The gathering of believers we met with were not questioned or harassed by any governmental group. There was no official state representative there to enforce regulations or impose boundaries on our worship service. In today's world that is a blessing, and a rarity among nations. At this point in our history we still have the freedom to worship the way we are called by God to praise Him.

We gathered again on Sunday evening to study and learn about each other and our Savior, Jesus Christ. There was no interference. We are free to worship, free to praise Him. This freedom does not go unnoticed, nor is it taken for granted. Thank you Lord for this miracle of freedom. Let your name forever be praised.

Bible Reference; Notes

1. Praise;

    <u>PS 9:1</u> – "I will give thanks to the Lord with all my heart…"

    <u>PS 25:1</u> – "To Thee, O Lord I lift up my soul. O my God, in Thee I trust."

    <u>PS 37:4</u> – "Delight yourself in the Lord; and He will give you the desires of your heart…"

2. Blessing;

    <u>PS 29:10-11</u> – "…Yes the Lord sits as King forever. The Lord will give strength to His people…"

    <u>PS 33:12</u> – "Blessed is the nation whose God is the Lord."

    <u>PS 34; 9-10</u> – "For to those who fear Him, there is no want….But they who seek the Lord shall not be in want of any good thing."

    <u>1 John 2: 24-25</u> – "So you must remain faithful to what you have been taught from the beginning. If you do you will continue to live in fellowship with the Son and with the Father. And in this fellowship we enjoy the eternal life (blessing) He promised us."

3. Fellowship;

    <u>Acts 2:42</u> – "They (those who believe) joined with the other believers and devoted themselves to the apostles' teaching and fellowship, sharing the Lord's Supper and in prayer."

    <u>Eph. 5:11</u> – "Take no part (fellowship) in the worthless deeds of evil and darkness; instead rebuke and expose them."

    <u>1 John 1:6</u> – "So we are lying if we say we have fellowship with God but go on living in Spiritual darkness. We are not living in the truth."

_____

_____

_____

_____

_____

_____

DAY 6

Once again Lord, you perform the miraculous in the seemingly small things of life. On the way to my work I looked up and saw our Nation's Flag proudly blowing in the wind.

In that small amount of time, as I passed it, I realized how much work and preparation You put into that moment of my life. It started with Adam and his broken covenant with You. Then there was Abraham and the New covenant. From there You dealt with Moses and the Law, the Ten Commandments, the manna, water from the rock, the bronze serpent, the parting of the Red Sea and then the final Covenant in Jesus the Christ, His death on the cross, my forgiveness and His resurrection, which all foreshadowed the covenant upon which my Nation was founded.

The noble experiment in democracy, righteous forefathers and the establishment of this nation's government are all based upon the God given Judeo-Christian inheritance You have provided for us. How could I have chosen my parents, my country? How is it that God called my name before I was born? By what miracle did I survive the experiences of childhood, being in harm's way during war time? Others did not survive, why was I blessed in such a manner? Who can account for my blessed marriage, children, personal welfare?

Praise be unto the God of Abraham! You provided. Thank You Father.

Bible Reference; Notes

1. The Covenant;

   <u>Gen 9:16</u> –"When I see the rainbow in the clouds, I will remember the eternal covenant between God and every living creature on earth." (God and Noah)

   <u>Gen. 17:7</u> –"I will continue this everlasting covenant between us, generation after generation. It will continue between me (God) and your (Abraham's) offspring forever…I will always be your God."

2. The New Covenant;

   <u>Heb.8:10</u> –"But this is the new covenant I will make with the people…on that day says the Lord. I will put my laws in their minds…I will write them on their hearts…I will be their God and they shall be my people."

   <u>Heb. 12:24</u> – "…Jesus, the one who mediates the new covenant between God and people…"

   <u>Heb. 13:20, 21</u>– "Now, may the God of peace who brought again from the dead our Lord Jesus equip you with all you need for doing his will…Jesus is the great Shepherd of the sheep (us) by an everlasting covenant, signed with his blood."

3. The Name;

   <u>Matt. 1:21</u> –"And she will have a son and you are to name him Jesus, for he will save his people…"

   <u>Acts 4:11-12</u> – "For Jesus is the one referred to in the Scriptures, where it says…has now become the cornerstone. There is salvation in no one else! There is no other name in all of heaven for people to call on to save them."

Kenneth L. Canion

———————————————————————

———————————————————————

———————————————————————

———————————————————————

———————————————————————

———————————————————————

DAY 7

I read in your word, "...be still and know that I am God, I will be exalted." Here I realize that any business which seems to shape my life is only hollow noise.

God, you are on your throne and will be exalted, regardless of what I do or think. I can always depend on You to be ever present, never changing, always true. You do not change; Your word does not change.

You God are the one thing I can count on to remain true, faithful, dependable, comforting and Holy. This is the miracle I receive every day. How could You have found a worm like me and prepared a place of eternal dwelling that is astoundingly desirable? Your word says that eye has not seen, ear has not heard nor has entered into the heart of man the things that you have prepared for them who love you.

Thank you Lord. Knowing your love for me is my daily blessing, regardless of my circumstances here on earth.

Bible References; Notes

1. Everlasting;

    Isa. 9:7 –"His ever expanding peaceful government will never end. He will rule forever with fairness and justice…"

    Isa. 40:28 –"Have you never heard or understood? Don't you know that the Lord is the everlasting God, the creator of all the earth?"

2. Exalted;

    PS 46:10 – "Be silent and know I am God! I will be honored by every nation. I will be honored throughout the world."

    PS 99:5 – "Exalt the Lord our God! Bow low before His feet, for He is Holy"

3. Worm/Change;

    PS 22:6 – "But I am a worm and not a man. I am scorned and despised by all!"

    2 Cor. 5:17 –"…Those who become Christians become new persons. They are not the same anymore, for the old life is gone. A new life is begun."

4. Trust;

    PS 25:1 – "To You O Lord, I lift up my soul. I trust in You my God. Do not let me be disgraced or let my enemies rejoice in my defeat."

    Rom. 8:38 – "And I am convinced that nothing can ever separate us from His love…nothing in all creation will ever be able to separate us from the love of God that is revealed in Christ Jesus Christ our Lord."

DAY 8

Last night we went to church. I was met and hugged and gave hugs to people. People are there who love me. I feel warm and safe there. No one tried to stop us from worshipping our Lord. It wasn't illegal to gather together in like fellowship and worship the Lord.

Our country, this Nation, was founded on the principle of religious freedom. To this point in our Nation's history it is still OK to worship and praise the Lord God Almighty. The efforts of a few Godly men in our Nation's history have paved the way for our worship last night.

There are places on this earth where what we did last night is illegal. Some people in this world are prosecuted for worshipping Jesus Christ. Some people are jailed and some killed for doing what we did last night. Except for the Grace of God, our Nation still allows its people to praise the Lord in public worship, free from governmental tyranny. Thank you Jesus!

Bible References; Notes

1. Worship;
   Luke 4:8 –"Jesus replied…You must worship the Lord your God; serve only Him."
   John 4:24 – "For God is Spirit, so those who worship Him must worship in spirit and in truth."
   PS 22:27-28 –"The whole earth will acknowledge the Lord and return to Him. People from every nation will bow down before Him (Worship Him). For the Lord is King. He rules all the nations."

2. Freedom;
   John 8:31-32 –"Jesus said…'You are truly my disciples if you keep obeying my teachings. And you know the truth, and the truth will set you free.'"
   Rom. 6:22 –"But now you are free from the power of sin and have become slaves of God. Now you do those things that lead to holiness and result in eternal life."
   2 Cor. 3:17 – "Now, the Lord is the Spirit, and wherever the Spirit of the Lord is, He gives freedom."

3. Joy;
   PS 33:12 –"What joy for the nations whose God is the Lord, whose people He has chosen for His own."
   Rom. 15:13 –"So I pray that God, who gives you hope, will keep you happy and full of peace as you believe in Him. May you overflow with hope (Joy) through the power of the Holy Spirit.
   Gal. 5:22 –"But when the Holy Spirit control our lives, He will produce this kind of fruit in us: love, joy, peace, patience, kindness, goodness, faithfulness, gentleness and self- control…"

Kenneth L. Canion

_____

_____

_____

_____

_____

_____

DAY 9

There is not a day that when I wake that God hasn't shown His mercy and grace in some way. Two things are on my mind this morning.

The freedom we enjoy in this country, so far, is amazing. Last night we decided to go to a Second Amendment political meeting. There we gathered with hundreds of other like-minded people. It was peaceful; there was no armed authority to control or listen to us. We were free to discuss and listen to those of like views. This surely is a blessing from God.

Years ago our Founding Fathers established a covenant relationship with the Lord God Almighty. He still blesses us because of that. (Our nation right now is not doing too good on honoring its part of that relationship.)

It is cold and wet outside and has been for several days. I am warm. I slept warm last night and am assured of sleeping warm again tonight. Every time I take a warm shower I praise the Lord. God has supplied my every need. He provides for my creature comfort. This is something we may tend to take for granted. I want to go on record now thanking Him for these, every day, seemingly mundane, blessings that He constantly pours into my life.

Bible References; Notes

1. Honor;

    Prov. 3:9-10 –"Honor the Lord with your wealth and with the best part of everything your land produces. Then He will fill your barns with grain and your vats will over flow…"

    John 5:23 – Jesus' words –"…honor the son just as they honor the Father. But if you refuse to honor the son, then you are certainly not honoring the father who sent Him."

    1 Tim. 1:17 –"Glory and honor to God forever and ever. He is the eternal King, the unseen one who never dies; He alone is God. Amen."

2. Needs;

    Matt. 6:8 – Jesus' words –"Don't be like them, because your Father knows exactly what you need even before you ask him!"

    Phil. 4:19 –"And this same God who takes care of me will supply all your needs from his glorious riches, which have been given to us in Christ Jesus."

    Matt. 6:32 –Jesus' words –"Why be like the pagans who are so deeply concerned about these things? Your heavenly father already knows all your needs."

3. Reign;

    PS 146:10 –"The Lord reigns forever…your God is King in every generation."

    Rom. 5:17 –"…but all who receive God's wonderful, gracious gift of righteousness will live (reign) in triumph over sin and death through this one man Jesus Christ."

    1 Cor.15:25-26 –"For Christ must reign until He humbles all enemies beneath His feet. And the last enemy to be destroyed is death."

_____

_____

_____

_____

_____

_____

DAY 10

Yesterday after work I took my sweetheart out for supper. Just consider the privileges in that! Let's consider what miracles God has done for me to be able to do that.

To begin with, I had a choice that doesn't exist in many lives: Going out to eat...a job that produces a salary with surplus income... A mode of transportation...Freedom to move about...A government that encourages private enterprise...The Food and Drug Administration works so well I don't even consider it a health risk to "eat out."

We were not accosted on the streets by outlaw gangs. The Department of Transportation gives us excellent roads, consistent laws and adequate enforcement. We weren't preyed upon by the government that is designed to protect us. I have a Concealed Handgun License so I broke no laws by being armed. There is no law to prevent us from discussing politics and expressing disagreement with our President. Our monetary system is dependable.

We came home, parked in our driveway and locked the doors, then went to bed. All done with reasonable expectation of status quo when we awake. God has performed and performs miracles in every aspect of my daily life! How can we complain?

Bible References; Notes

1. Provision;
   > <u>Job 38:41</u> –"Who provides food for the ravens when their young cry out to God as they wander a bout in hunger?" Won't God do much more for us?
   >
   > <u>PS 68:19</u> – "Praise the Lord; praise God our savior! For each day He carries us in His arms."
   >
   > <u>Luke 11:3</u> – "This is how you should pray…Give us our food day by day…"

2. Gifts;
   > <u>Ecc. 3:13</u> –"…people should eat and drink and enjoy the fruits of their labor, for these are gifts from God."
   >
   > <u>Matt. 7:11</u> – "If you sinful people know how to give good gifts to your children, how much more will your heavenly Father give good gifts (the Holy Spirit) to those who ask Him."
   >
   > <u>James 1:17</u> – "Whatever is good and perfect comes to us from God above…"

3. Protection;
   > <u>Matt. 4:6</u> – (His children receive the same protection as Jesus Christ.) "…For the scriptures say, He orders His angels to protect you…"
   >
   > <u>PS 34:4</u> -"I prayed to the Lord, and He answered me, freeing (protecting) me from all my fears."
   >
   > <u>PS 91:9, 10</u> – "If you make the Lord your refuge, if you make the Most High your shelter, no evil will conquer you."

_____

_____

_____

DAY 11

God is good in His daily provisions all the time. His provision for us repeats itself so often that we tend to take it for granted. When food is prepared and just before we eat, my mind is overwhelmed with all the times we sat and ate.

We fill our stomach over and over. It occurs with such regularity and is so consistent and happens with not a whole lot of effort on our part. He fills our mouths constantly! God is so great!

I consider who and what I am on this earth and am eternally amazed that He chose to bless me like this. I really don't understand it, but I do appreciate it. Not only does He give me sustenance, He provides a variety. I have a choice of what and how much to eat. My God is mighty. He provides for mind, body and soul on a continual, consistent basis!

My prayer is for everyone to be as blessed as I am, for everyone to fill their belly with the same regularity as I do. Truly God has and is blessing this family in a supernatural way! Blessed be the name of the Lord!

Bible References; Notes

1. Provision

    <u>Matt. 5:6</u> – "Blessed are those who hunger and thirst for righteousness, for they shall be filled."

    <u>Luke 1:53</u> –"He has filled (provided for) the hungry with good things…"

    <u>Rom.15:13</u> –"So I pray that God, who gives you hope (provides for you) will keep you happy and full of peace as you believe in him."

2. Faithfulness;

    <u>PS 119:90</u> –"Thy faithfulness continues throughout all generations;"

    <u>1 Cor.1:9</u> –"God will surely do this for you, for he always does what he says (is faithful) and he is the one who invited you into this wonderful friendship with his Son, Jesus Christ our Lord."

    <u>1 John 1:9</u> –"But if we confess our sins to him, he is faithful and just to forgive us and to cleanse us from every wrong."

3. Blessed

    <u>Deu. 2:7</u> –"The Lord your God has blessed everything you have done and has watched your every step…"

    <u>PS 18:46</u> –"The Lord lives! Blessed be my Rock! May the God of my salvation be exalted!"

    <u>PS 33:12</u> –"Blessed is the nation whose God is the Lord."

    <u>Matt. 11:6</u> – Jesus' words –"And blessed is he whosoever shall not be offended in me."

_____

_____

_____

_____

DAY 12

This was a beautiful day. Today the glory of the sun was seen. After days of rain and cloudy weather we got to enjoy the light and warmth of the sun.

"The heavens declare the glory of God and the earth shows His handiwork." Whether a person is a believer or not he can still enjoy the things that God has created. So, what is the big deal about a pretty day?

We have life to enjoy. Our sense of feel, touch, sight and hearing are all in place. There is no oppression to kill our enjoyment. It (the beautiful day) is a way that God testifies to us that He is the creator and is still "on the Throne."

In addition, today we worshipped God freely at the church of our choice. (Not all countries allow their people to do that.) God received our praises and gave us joy and blessings. We were able to meet with friends and spend time with them. There was no fear in our conversation; no one monitored what we said. We ate food other people prepared without worry for health reasons. We had money to pay for it. We have reasonable expectations that we can work to replace the money spent. We met in small groups Sunday evening to study and discuss the Word of God, no one tried to stop us!

Bible References; Notes

1. Good Things;

    PS 19:1 – "The Heavens declare the glory of God… There is no speech nor are there words where *their* voice is not heard."

    Matt. 7:11 –"If you then, being evil, know how to give good gifts to your children, how much more shall your Father who is in heaven give what is good to those who ask Him."

    Matt. 5:45 –"…for He causes His sun to rise on the evil and the good, and sends rain on the righteous and the unrighteous."

2. Creator;

    Col. 1:16 –"For by Him all things were created, both in the heavens and on earth, visible and invisible… all things…"

    1 Peter 4:19 –"…keep on doing what is right, and trust yourself to the God who made you (Creator), for he will never fail you."

    Rev. 4:11 –"…for You created all things, and because of your will they existed and were created."

3. Worship;

    Deu. 11:16 –"But do not let your heart turn away from the Lord to worship other gods."

    PS 29:2 –"Give honor to the Lord for the glory of his name. Worship the Lord in the splendor of his holiness."

    Heb. 10:25 –"…not forsaking our own assembling together, encouraging one another, as you see the day drawing near."

_____

_____

_____

_____

_____

DAY 13

The Lord gave us a beautiful day today. This day was available for everyone, both the just and the unjust.

Because of the awareness, the world view that I have in Christ it was much more than just a pretty day. Even the deer knew this day was different from the rainy, cloudy days that we normally have this time of year. So in that we are alike.

The awareness that God has placed in those of us that have been redeemed gives us a view, a glimpse of creation and life that is dim to those without the Holy Spirit in their life.

It is a one way vision for the unsaved, but like a two way mirror for those whom Christ has called and redeemed. Man, in the natural, doesn't wonder about what he can't see, but man under the Grace of God can realize that his vision of life has been expanded and can recall what he wasn't aware of before salvation.

I am in this state of awareness not because of anything I have earned on my own. God called me to this Grace through Jesus Christ His Son. Praise the Lord!

Bible Reference; Notes

1. Sight;

    <u>Isa. 43:4</u> –"Others have died that you might live. I traded their lives for yours because you are precious (in my sight) to me. You are honored and I love you."

    <u>I Cor. 13:12</u> –"For now we see in a mirror dimly, but then face to face; now I know in part, but then I shall know fully just as I also have been fully known."

    <u>Col. 1:22</u> –"You were his (Jesus') enemies…yet now he has brought you back as his friends. He brought you into the very presence (sight) of God, and you are holy and blameless."

2. Oneness;

    <u>I Cor. 12:12</u> –"For even as the body is one and yet has many members, and all the members of the body, though many, are one body, so also is Christ."

    <u>I Cor. 12:27</u> –"Now all of you together are Christ's Body, and each one of you is a separate and necessary part of it."

    <u>Eph. 4:3</u> –"Always keep yourselves united in the Holy Spirit and bind yourselves together in peace."

3. Awareness;

    <u>Eph. 2:4,5</u> –"But God is so rich in mercy, and He loved us so very much, that even while we were dead because of our sins, He gave us life when He raised Christ from the dead."

    <u>Eph. 2:9</u> –"Salvation is not a reward for the good things we have done, so none of us can boast."

_____

_____

DAY 14

God is delightful and trustworthy. He can be trusted to do what His word says He will do, just believe. God said it, that settles it, regardless whether I believe it or not.

I am having, have been having, trouble with my right shoulder. I'm talking major pain here. On several occasions I have spent the night in a chair because the pain was so excruciating that I could not lie down. Doctor visits and MRI's show that I have pinched nerves in my neck, along the fifth and sixth vertebra. They also reveal bone spurs on my shoulder socket. For some reason neither the orthopedic surgeon nor the spine doctor want to do anything. So, I attend physical therapy twice a week.

During revival services last night, the speaker described my symptoms. She then asked for the person with those symptoms to come forward. I did so. Two male ministers came and laid hands on me. I agreed with them and did not resist the Holy Spirit but joined with them in praising Him. Last night I slept all night through without being awakened by pain even once! I spent the previous night in a recliner due to the pain of lying down.

I love it when the Word of God destroys all sense of logic and human reasoning.

Bible Reference; Notes

1. Word;

    PS 107:20 –"He sent His word and healed them, and delivered them…"

    PS 119:105 –"Thy word is a lamp to my feet and a light to my path."

    Matt. 4:4 –"It is written, man shall not live on bread alone, but on every word that proceeds out of the mouth of God."

    John 1:1 –"In the beginning was the Word, and the Word was with God, and the Word was God. He was in the beginning with God."

2. Truth;

    John 4:23 – Jesus' words –"The time is coming and is here when true worshipers will worship the Father in spirit and in truth. (He) is looking for anyone who will worship Him that way."

    John 17:16-17 –"They are not of the world, even as I am not of the world. Sanctify them in the truth. Thy word is truth."

    1 John 3 –"May grace, mercy and peace, which comes from God our Father and from Jesus Christ his son, be with us who live in truth and love."

3. Alive;

    Heb. 4:12 –"For the word of God is living and active and sharper than any two-edged sword…"

    2 Tim. 2:15 –"Be diligent to present yourself approved to God as a workman who does not need to be ashamed, handling accurately the word of Truth."

_____

_____

_____

_____

_____

DAY 15

God blesses us again and again. I can't take for granted how He repeats His blessings on a daily basis. Every time we get sleepy a warm, safe, comfortable place to rest is available. Every time bills come in there is money available to pay them. Every time we need to go somewhere there is a vehicle waiting to serve us. Every time it gets dark I can flip a switch and bring forth light.

I can call on the phone anytime, to anywhere I want. Water to drink or bathe is available at the twist of a knob. I have the freedom to listen to any radio station I want. I can agree or disagree with any political commentator. I have freedom of speech and freedom to worship. No one interferes with my personal expressions of faith in my God.

These things do not occur naturally in the realm of humankind. This country and I have been blessed with these freedoms primarily because of the covenant relationship with Almighty God, established by the founders of this great nation.

Of these things I am aware, and very grateful. I rue the day when we as a nation no longer honor God in this relationship, when we stop being His people.

Bible References; Notes

1. Condition;

   <u>2 Chron. 7:14</u> –"If my people who are called by my Name will humble themselves and pray and seek my face and turn from their wicked ways, then I will hear from heaven, will forgive their sin, and will heal their land."

   <u>Matt4:4</u> –"But He answered and said, It is written, Man shall not live on bread alone, but on every word that proceeds out of the mouth of God."

2. Word;

   <u>PS 56:4</u> –"O God, I praise your word. I trust in God, so why should I be afraid? What can mere mortals do to me?"

   <u>Luke 11:28</u> –Jesus' words –"On the contrary, blessed are those who hear the word of God and observe it."

   <u>Col.3:16</u> –"Let the word of Christ richly dwell within you…"

3. Action;

   <u>Prov. 16:3</u> –"Commit your work to the Lord and then your plans will succeed."

   <u>Eph. 2:10</u> –"For we are God's masterpiece. He has created us anew in Christ Jesus, so that we can do the good things (work) he planned for us long ago.'

   <u>2 Tim.2:15</u> –"Be diligent to present yourself approved to God as a workman who does not need to be ashamed, handling accurately the word of truth."

DAY 16

This morning I am in the "pit" of despair. God hasn't failed me, nor will He ever. His love is as continuous as the air we breathe. It is there for the taking. It is so present and in such quantity that we often take it for granted. We forget that our participation in His love cost Him dearly. "For God so loved the world that He gave…" He suffered tremendously to get us to redemption, praise His Holy Name.

My problem is that I leave the covenant, I break the agreement. When I do, the disappointment in me is so great as to lead to depression. It is my human side, my carelessness in handling God's word. I always believe it, I don't always follow it.

Every time I step out from under His Grace I am stung with great regret and shame. How can mankind continue to "sin" and still be accepted by our Lord? Thank God, His Grace is in abundant supply and never fails us. God is merciful and just and not only cleanses us of our present sin, but of all that we have done.

Whereas I am still grieving for my display of anger in my classroom, I know that Jesus has covered all my sin and will restore me.

Bible Reference; Notes

1. Despair;

    Deu. 31:8 – "Do not be afraid or discouraged, for the Lord is the one who goes before you; He will be with you. He will never fail you nor forsake you."

    PS 27:1 – "The Lord is my light and my salvation so why should I be afraid? The Lord protects me from danger, so why should I tremble?"

    2 Cor. 4:8 – "We are pressed on every side by troubles, but we are not crushed or broken. We are perplexed, but we don't give up and quit."

2. Forgiveness;

    PS 32:5 – "I acknowledged my sin to you...I will confess my transgressions to the Lord. You forgave me the guilt and iniquity of my sins."

    Eph. 1:7 – "He (God) is so rich in kindness that he purchased our freedom through the blood of his Son and our sins are forgiven."

    Col. 3:13 – "...and forgiving each other..., just as the Lord forgave you..."

3. Grace;

    Rom. 6:14 – "For sin shall not be master over you, for you are not under law, but under grace."

    Eph. 2:8, 9 – "For by grace you have been saved through faith; and that not of yourselves, it is the gift of God not of works, lest any man should boast."

    1 Peter 5:10 – "In his kindness (Grace) God called you to his eternal glory by means of Jesus Christ."

_____

_____

_____

_____

DAY 17

God has restored me. I am grateful for His restoration. I constantly judge myself and am more often than not lacking in my estimation of myself. God is faithful. He is the ultimate judge. It is His word that counts. God has spoken in His Word and it is always true, always right, regardless of what I think or say.

I know God restores me, His word says, "If my people (me) who are called by My name will humble themselves (me) and pray, and seek my face and turn from their wicked ways, then will I hear their prayer (mine) from heaven, forgive their sins (mine) and heal their land (life)." Since this is in His word, I have no right to continue the self-condemnation. His Word says it, and that settles it. Whether I believe it or not makes no difference.

Tonight we had a good revival service. We just finished up a week of "Prayer-revival" service. I have learned to become bolder in my faith. I learned to focus better. It is like when I take my glasses off I can still see, but when I put them on, oh how much better. God has focused my life like that. Put the Holy Spirit on and our focus becomes much better. We can see, but the Holy Spirit brings a much sharper focus!

Bible Reference; Notes

1. Restoration;
    PS 23:1&3 –"The Lord is my shepherd; I have everything I need. He lets me rest in green meadows; He leads me beside peaceful streams, He renews (restores) my strength."

    PS 31:24 –"So be strong and take courage, all you who put your hope in the Lord."

    Jer. 29:11 –"For I know the plans I have for you says the Lord. They are plans for good and not for disaster, to give you a future and a hope in the Lord."

2. Faithful;
    PS 31:23 –"Love the Lord all you faithful ones. For the Lord protects all those who are loyal to Him, but he harshly punishes all who are arrogant."

    2 Thes. 3:3 –"But the Lord is faithful, and He will strengthen and protect you from the evil one."

    1 John 1:9 –"If we confess our sins, He is faithful and just to forgive us our sins…cleanse us from all unrighteousness."

3. Word;
    Matt. 4:4 –"…man shall not live on bread alone, but every word that proceeds out of the mouth of God."

    Luke 11:28 –"…blessed are those who hear the word of God and observe it."

    1 Peter 1:23 –"…for you have been born again… through…the word of God."

DAY 18

Today I had the task of preparing my income tax records. I often get angry or frustrated when doing so. Then I remember that I live protected by this government, the one I am preparing to pay. I am blessed by this form of government in several ways.

God has blessed me in the fact that I have an income. I have the freedom to purchase a house, a car, and have a lifestyle that the majority of the people in the world do not have. I realize that by paying these taxes, my fair share, the government stays in operation.

God has blessed me with this country, this government, this way of life. I didn't choose my parents, my place or time of birth, my intellect or my health. Everything I am or have is a gift from our Creator. I am made like I am made; I had nothing to do with it. He knew me before I was formed; He called my name before I was born. What can I say, what can I take credit for? God loves me because. It is His nature, His desire and His plan. I can only be thankful for such a Creator as He!

Bible Reference; Notes

1. Government;
   > Isa. 9:6 –"…a son will be given unto us and the government will rest upon His shoulders…"
   > Rom. 13:1 –"Obey the government, for God is the one who put it there. All governments have been placed in power by God. So those who refuse to obey the laws of the land are refusing to obey God and punishment will follow."

2. Knowledge;
   > Ecc.2:26 –"God gives wisdom, knowledge and joy to those who please him."
   > Jer. 1:5 –"Before I formed you in the womb I knew you…"
   > John 6:64 –"But there are some of you who do not believe. For Jesus, from the beginning knew (had knowledge of) who they were who did not believe…"

3. Love;
   > John 3:16 –"For God so loved the world that He gave…"
   > 1 John 4:10,11,19 –"…He loved us and sent His Son to die for us…if God so loved us we ought to love one another…we love because He first loved us."
   > Gal. 5:13-14 –"For you have been called to live in freedom – not freedom to satisfy your sinful nature, but freedom to serve one another in love. For the whole law can be summed up in this one command; Love your neighbor as yourself."

Kenneth L. Canion

_____

_____

_____

_____

DAY 19

God has revealed much to me this week, and on this evening He showed me another aspect of His Grace. During the Prayer Revival I went to the front of the church in response to a call from the evangelist who was not aware of the pain I was having in my shoulder. (…pinched nerve and slightly torn rotator cuff.). As people prayed and laid hands on me, for a moment I went completely blank mentally. For a second or so I was unaware of anything about me. In my mind I have always had a tendency to criticize others for "falling out", now I don't.

Today (Sunday) I was caught by a fit of laughter that overcame me while I was singing in church. It was so refreshing, so releasing, and so joyful. It was a deep laughter that brought tears to my eyes. It didn't cause a scene or disturb anyone. It was tremendously enjoyable to me. It was just a "thing" between me and the Holy Spirit.

This evening in college class at the church, toward the end, when we were closing, a feeling of profound sadness overcame me. I felt led to ask the college class to go to a member and pray for her because I felt the sadness she had in her. As they were praying with her I began to cry over what was happening in her life. She told the ladies what was going on with her. They gathered around her and prayed for healing and the Peace that passes all understanding.

I can never doubt the movement of the Holy Spirit in my life again.

Bible Reference; Notes

1. Prayer;

    Isa. 56:7 –"…For My house will be called a house of prayer for all the people."

    Phil. 4:6 –"Be anxious for nothing, but in everything by prayer and supplication with thanksgiving let your requests be made known to God."

    James 5:16 –"…pray for one another, so that you may be healed. The effective prayer of a righteous man can accomplish much."

2. Signs;

    Isa. 7:14 –"…the Lord himself will choose a sign. Look! The virgin will conceive a child, she will give birth to a son and will call him Immanuel – God is with us."

    I Cor. 14:22 –"So you see that speaking in tongues is a sign, not for the believers, but for unbelievers; prophecy, however, is for the benefit of believers not unbelievers."

3. Cry;

    PS 34:17 –"The righteous cry and the Lord hears and delivers them out of all their troubles."

    Matt. 26:75 –"Suddenly Jesus' words flashed through Peter's mind…and he went away crying (weeping) bitterly."

    John 11:35 –"Then Jesus wept."

    Luke 6:21 –"…Blessed are you who hunger now… blessed are you who weep now…for you shall laugh."

_____

_____

_____

_____

_____

DAY 20

When I am tempted to say this was just another day, I must remember that my God is the creator of this Universe and everything that is in it! It is a miracle that I even exist. It is a miracle that He decided to single me out of all humanity to call my name and instill in me the divine spark of life eternal.

Consider every human being who ever lived on this earth. Whatever that number would be is huge! Then consider just one individual, one single dot in the middle of that vast multitude. That dot, that speck is me. He called my name out. He offered Himself upon that cross, He faced the greatest humility of all and He died to set me free! All this was done without any effort on my part. I wasn't even looking for Him. He just did it because of His great love for mankind.

I can't imagine! I haven't the slightest clue of the depth of His love for me. At times in my life I've tried to ignore Him, to reject Him, to deny Him. Each time His gentle voice calls me back. He loves me, and there is nothing I can do about it! I just bask is His love and am continually grateful that He chose me.

With a creator like this there is no way a person can wake up each morning without seeing that every second surrounded by His love is a miracle!

Bible Reference; Notes

1. Created;

   <u>PS 148:5</u> —"Let every created thing give praise to the Lord, for he has issued his command and they came into being."

   <u>Isa. 41:20</u> —"Everyone will see this miracle (water in the desert) and understand that it is the Lord, the Holy One of Israel, who did (created) it."

   <u>Col. 1:16</u> —"Christ is the one through whom God created everything in heaven and earth. He made the things we can see and the things we can't see — kings, kingdoms rulers and authorities. Everything has been created through him and for him."

2. Called;

   <u>Rom. 8:28</u> —"And we know that God causes all things to work together for good to those who love God and are called according to His purpose."

   <u>1 Thes. 2:12</u> —"...live your lives in a way that God would consider worthy. For he called you into his Kingdom to share his glory."

   <u>Heb. 9:15b</u> —"...those who have been called may receive the promise of eternal inheritance."

3. Persuaded;

   <u>Rom. 8:38,39</u> —"For I am persuaded that neither death, nor life, nor angels, nor principalities, nor things present, not things to come, nor powers, nor height, nor depth, nor any other created thing, shall be able to separate us from the love of God, which is in Christ Jesus our Lord."

<u>2 Tim. 1:12</u> – Paul's words –"And that is why I am suffering here in prison. But I am not ashamed of it, for I know that the one in whom I trust and I am sure (persuaded) that he is able to guard what I have entrusted to him (Jesus) until the day of his return."

_____

_____

_____

_____

_____

_____

DAY 21

God is concerned about our physical health. He is the basis of our physical well- being. My sweetie (wife) went for a medical check-up today. Nothing was suspected by either one of us, just a routine follow-up appointment. She called me from the Doctor's office in tears saying she wanted to come home right then instead of running some other errands. She needed to be with me.

That is special, when someone else wants and depends on you. I said to come on home and let's talk. (Praise the Lord!) The blessed part is for a person to have a soul mate to be comforted by when physical problems arise. God has blessed us in that way. I was worried, had a heavy heart, thinking all sorts of things, wondering if there was something seriously wrong. I came to find out that the blood drawing process she went through was extra painful and she just wanted to be comforted because of the pain.

Thank You Lord for a beautifully healthy mate that cares for me and is comforted by being in my presence! In the act of comforting and reassuring her, I too drew warmth and a sense of belonging and importance, because of the love of the Father and the fact that I was needed and wanted by my partner.

Bible Reference; Notes

1. Marriage;

   <u>Matt. 19:4-5</u> –"…from the beginning God made them male and female…This explains why a man leaves his father and mother and is joined to his wife and the two are united into one."

   <u>Mark 10:8-9</u> –"…since they are no longer two, but one, let no one separate them, for God has joined them together."

   <u>Heb. 13:4</u> –"Give honor to marriage, and remain faithful to one another in marriage."

2. Comfort;

   <u>PS 23:4</u> –"Even when I walk through the dark valley of death I will not be afraid for you are close beside me, your rod and your staff protect and comfort me."

   <u>1 Thes.5:11</u> –"So encourage (comfort) each other and build each other up, just as you are already doing."

   <u>2 Thes.2:16-17</u> –"May or Lord Jesus Christ and God our Father, who loved us and in His special favor gave us everlasting comfort and good hope comfort your hearts and give you strength in every good thing you do and say."

3. Renewal;

   <u>PS 51:10</u> –"Create in me a clean heart, O God. Renew a right spirit within me."

   <u>Isa. 40:31</u> –"Yet those who wait for the Lord will gain new strength (be renewed); they will mount up with wings like eagles. They will run and not get tired. They will walk and not become weary."

<u>Heb. 6:4-6</u> –"For it is impossible to restore to repentance (renew) those who were once enlightened – experienced the good things of heaven – shared in the Holy Spirit – tasted the goodness of the Word of God – and who then turn away from God."

_____

_____

_____

_____

_____

_____

DAY 22

God is miraculously ordinary in so many ways. What seems to be an ordinary day turns miraculous when seen through spiritual eyes.

Using the earthquake in Haiti would be a good comparison. Here at home I stand in the shower under warm refreshing water. All I have to do is turn it on. I have clothes in the closet, a room, a house. Death and destruction do not surround me. My country's infrastructure is in place. Traffic lights work, electricity is available to me at the flip of a switch. The laws of the land are effective, there is no open looting, I can depend upon having protection when traversing the roads, going to and from work, and my wife is safe at home waiting for my return. Today I even voted in the process of deciding which lawmakers to put into office.

The other night I even left my front door unlocked all night. No worry, no problem. His angels take charge over me. I sleep in comfort and security. O God, how blessed I am. You never fail to watch over me. Great and Holy is Your name. Blessed be the name of the Lord.

Bible Reference; Notes

1. Protection;

    <u>Gen 24:40</u> –"And he said unto me…The Lord… will send His angel with you to make your journey successful…"

    <u>PS 91:1-3</u> –"He who dwells in the shelter of the Most High will abide in the shadow of the Almighty. I will say to the Lord, my refuge and my fortress, my God in whom I trust, for it is He who delivers…"

    <u>Luke 4:10</u> –"For it is written, He will give His angels charge concerning you."

2. Spiritual eyesight;

    <u>Acts 26:18</u> –"…to open their eyes that they might turn from darkness to light and from the dominion of Satan to God in order that they may receive forgiveness of sins…"

    <u>Eph. 1:18</u> –"…that the eyes of your heart may be enlightened so that you may know…the hope of His calling…the riches of His glory of our inheritance… the surpassing greatness of His power toward those of us who believe, according to the working of the strength of His might."

3. Safety;

    <u>PS 4:8</u> –"I will lie down in peace and sleep, for you alone Lord will keep me safe."

    <u>Hosea 2:18</u> –"In that day I will also make a covenant for them…and will make them lie down in safety."

_____

_____

_____

_____

DAY 23

Yesterday we heard the news of another killer quake. This time it was in Chile, an 8.8 on the Rector Scale. In Haiti more than 200 thousand died after or because of the earthquake. The death toll in San Diego, Chile has not yet been determined. Amid this devastation, here I sit, all safe and comfortable. Our water, utilities and life style go on uninterrupted.

Is this because of my righteousness? Does God like me better? Absolutely not. We are blessed because of our location on the globe. It is so hard to reason out the whys and wherefores of great tragedies like this. These are natural phenomena that occur in God's perfect timing. It is all known to God, every hair on our head is numbered. God is completely sovereign, there is no unknown disaster waiting to descend upon mankind. Everything has a consequence, things happen. However, nothing happens outside of God's knowledge or will. He has promised to take us through problems, not around them.

He has already warned or informed us of the events that would occur close to His return to this earth. Our thoughts, desires and actions, and our whereabouts in following His will controls our placement on this earth. Whenever we are included in such a tragedy, it is not random. Our God knows exactly what is going on and will always be there to guide us through.

Bible Reference; Notes

1. Abiding;

    John 15:5 –"I am the vine, you are the branches; he who abides in Me and I in him, he bears much fruit; for apart from me you can do nothing."

    John 15:10 –"If you keep my commandments you will abide in my love; just as I have kept My Father's commandments and abide in His love."

2. Fear;

    Isa. 54:17 –"No weapon formed against you shall prosper."

    PS 91:5-7 –"You will not be afraid of (fear) the terror by night or of the arrow that flies by day, or the pestilence that stalks in darkness or the destruction that lays waste at noon. A thousand shall fall at your side and ten thousand at your right hand; but it shall not approach you."

    Luke 21:11-19 – Summary –"There will be great earthquakes…famines…epidemics…terrifying things…miraculous signs in heaven…a time of great persecution. So don't worry (fear) not a hair on your head will perish. By standing firm you will win your souls."

3. Persuaded;

    Rom. 8:38 –"For I am persuaded that neither death nor life, nor angels, nor principalities, nor things present, nor things to come, nor powers, nor height nor depth, nor any other created thing shall be able to separate us from the love of God, which is in Christ Jesus our Lord."

    2 Tim. 1:12 –"…but I am not ashamed for I know whom I have believed and am persuaded that He is able to keep that which I've committed unto Him against that day."

_____

_____

_____

_____

_____

_____

DAY 24

Freedom in the Lord produces boldness in our character. Loving the Lord in my heart and letting that love overflow into boldness has been, to me, quite difficult. I've always felt that one's personal feelings is just that, personal.

God has been blessing me lately with a kind of boldness in declaring His name. Prior to this I guess my hesitancy has been out of fear, which is a good weapon used by Satan to thwart the Christian witness. Anyway, my wife and I were walking in the neighborhood yesterday and found out that our neighbor was scheduled for surgery on Monday. The Holy Spirit prompted me to ask him if we could pray right then. He was glad to do so. It was great, my neighbor felt he "needed that" and began to have a more positive attitude about his coming event.

In class tonight I was prompted again by the Holy Spirit to pray with/for a class member who was caught up in self-doubt and worry because of her physical and spiritual condition. I was moved with compassion. The class joined in and she was relieved and blessed with the assurance that God knows and cares for each one of us. She called upon Him, He rescued her. Her mind was set at peace.

Because I was in each of those places at the right time with the right message, I know God's timing is perfect and that He works through us if we will yield to His callings.

Bible Reference; Notes

1. Eye;

    PS 34:15 –"The eyes of the Lord are toward the righteous…His ears are open to their cry."

    PS 101:6 –"My eyes shall be upon the faithful…that they may dwell with me."

    1 Cor. 2:9 –"…No eye has seen, nor ear has heard and no mind has imagined what God has prepared for those who live Him."

2. Witness;

    John 15:26-27 – Jesus' words –"But I will send you the Counselor – the Spirit of truth. He will come to you from the Father and tell you about me. And you must also tell others about me…"

    Acts 22:15 –"You are to take His message everywhere, telling the whole world what you have seen and heard…why delay? Get up."

    Titus 1:2 –"This truth (witness) gives them the confidence of eternal life, which God promised them before the world began – and He cannot lie."

3. Call;

    PS 81:7 –"…you called in trouble and I rescued you."

    Isa. 54:17 – We are called of the Lord, therefore – "But in that coming day no weapon turned against you will succeed…"

    Acts 2:21 –"And it shall be that everyone who calls on the name of the Lord shall be saved."

_____

_____

_____

_____

_____

_____

DAY 25

"Beware of the Ides of March." Caesar had reason to fear. We have moved into March. This date sounds like science fiction to me. Haiti has had an earthquake, 250,000 causalities. Chile has had an earthquake, many killed, thousands homeless. Our Nation is a disaster financially. Our leadership, it seems, is "hell bent" on reducing us to a third world nation by out of control spending and massive growth in the size of the Federal Government.

Fear, this spells fear. The Bible tells us that perfect love casts out all fear. God has blessed us with perfect love. Fear has been cast out. We are free to live without fear of what may happen to us! God is in control, what can mere man do to us?

That is so great! Living without fear is truly a blessing from God. His Grace sustains us daily. No matter what happens, no matter where I am, God is there delivering me from fear. Fear can debilitate people. My God prevents that. Fear drives out joy. God has filled me with joy. The kind of joy God gives has nothing to do with the external condition of my life. Joy is deep inside, dictated to by the Holy Spirit who dwells there. Thank you God for this blessing! Thank you Jesus for dying for me, in my place. No fear!

Bible Reference; Notes

1. Harm;

   <u>1Chron.16:22</u> – God warned the nations on our behalf –"Do not touch these people I have chosen and do not hurt (harm) my prophets."

   <u>Jer. 29:11</u> –"For I know the plans I have for you, declares the Lord, plans for welfare and not for calamity (harm) to give you a future and a hope."

   <u>1 Peter 3:13</u> –"Now who will want to harm you if you are eager to do good?"

2. Joy;

   <u>1 Peter 4:13</u>- "But rejoice that you participate in the sufferings of Christ so that you may have joy when His glory is revealed."

   <u>Heb. 12:2</u> –"Let us fix our eyes upon Jesus, the author and perfector of our faith, who for the joy set before Him endured the cross, …" for us.

   <u>James 1</u>:2 –"Consider it all joy…when you encounter various trials knowing that the testing of your faith produces endurance."

3. Substitute;

   <u>Rom. 3:25</u> –"For God sent Jesus to take the punishment for our sins and to satisfy God's anger against us."

   <u>1 John 2:2</u> –"He (Jesus) is the atoning sacrifice (substitute) for our sins, and not only for ours but also for the sins of the whole world."

   <u>1 John 4:10</u> –"This is real love. It is not that we loved God, but that He loved us and sent His Son as a sacrifice (substitute) to take away our sins."

_____

_____

_____

_____

_____

DAY 26

Oh Lord my God there are a thousand things with which you bless me daily. My heart, my breath, my eyes, my life, my mate.

When I consider the works of your hands, the sun, the moon, the stars, I wonder what is man that you considered me. The fowls of the air , the beasts of the field, the fish of the sea and whatsoever passes through the paths of the sea, what is man that you consider him?

Forever God, I will be grateful to you. You called my name before I was born. I wasn't even looking for you! My God and my Lord, how excellent is your name in all the earth. I am overwhelmed when I think on these things. I know who I am, my sins are not hidden. Yet somehow you continue to love and bless me. In your place I wouldn't. You see something redeemable in me. You are always faithful, never tiring. It is too great for me to imagine. My eyes have not seen, ears have not heard, neither has entered into my heart the things you have prepared for me, if I but love you!

I live a privileged life Father. It is not because of my righteousness, it is because of the Grace of God through the sacrifice of Jesus Christ my Lord and Savior. Praise the Lord!

Bible reference; Notes

1. Blessed;

   PS 2:12b –"How blessed are all who take refuge in Him."

   PS 33:12 –"Blessed is the nation whose God is the Lord."

   PS 128:1 –"How blessed is everyone who fears the Lord, who walks in His ways."

2. Excellent;

   PS 8:1 –"O Lord our Lord, how majestic (excellent) is Thy name in all the earth…"

   PS 36:7 –"How priceless (excellent) is your unfailing love O God! All humanity finds shelter in the shadow of your wings."

   2 Peter 1:17 –"And He received honor and glory from God the Father when God's glorious … voice called down from heaven – 'This is my beloved Son; I am fully pleased with Him."

3. Sacrifice;

   Rom. 5:8 –"But God demonstrates His own love toward us, in that while we were yet sinners, Christ died for us."

   Heb. 9:26b –"But now He has appeared once for all… to do away with sin by the sacrifice of Himself."

   1Peter 2:24 –"…He himself bore our sins in His body on the cross…by His wounds we are healed."

   _____

   _____

   _____

_____

_____

_____

DAY 27

This day was Wednesday. We were able to go to church and get re-charged for the week. We got to be with our "family" members. We saw and greeted those whom we love and those who love us. It is in a retreat like this that daily wounds are healed. Here we can escape from the insanity of the world that we live in, to be in the world that is real, that will last.

In our Wednesday night world God reigns. The ugliness, the hatefulness of the temporary world is exposed for what it is. It is a world dominated by the "natural" ethics of mankind, where each individual considers himself the center of the universe. Nothing could be farther from the truth.

The truth is that Christ is the center, it is all about Him. It is not about us. He is at the center. We were made to praise Him, not ourselves. The word brought to us by our pastor was just what my injured heart needed. Where else, Lord, can a man turn for nurture and healing other than your word? Thank you God for supplying all my needs, the physical as well as the spiritual. Your word is a medicine unto my soul, sweetness unto my heart. Thank you so much.

Kenneth L. Canion

Bible reference; Notes

1. Foundation;

   <u>Isa. 48:12-13</u> –"Listen to me...I alone am God, the First and the Last (Alpha and Omega). It was my hand that laid the foundations of the earth. The palm of my right hand spread out the heavens above. I spoke and they came into being."

   <u>Luke 6:49</u> – Jesus' words –"but anyone who listens and doesn't obey is like a person who builds a house without a foundation."

   <u>Heb. 1:10-12</u> –"In the beginning, Lord, you laid the foundations of the earth and the heavens are the work of your hands. Even they will perish, but you remain forever."

2. Cornerstone;

   <u>PS 118:22</u> –"The stone rejected by the builders has now become the cornerstone."

   <u>Luke 6:47-48</u> – Jesus' words –"I will show you what it is like when someone comes to me, listens to my teaching and then obeys me. It is like a person who builds a house on a strong foundation laid upon the underlying rock." (Cornerstone, Jesus)

   <u>Eph. 2:20</u> –"We are his house, built on the foundation of the apostles and the prophets. And the cornerstone is Christ Jesus himself."

3. Reigns;

   <u>Exo. 15:18</u> –"The Lord will reign forever and ever."

   <u>Rom. 5:21</u> –"So just as sin ruled (reigned) over all people and brought them to death, now God's wonderful kindness rules (reigns) instead, giving us right standing with God and resulting in eternal life through Jesus Christ our Lord."

Eph. 3:14-15 —"For this reason I kneel before the Father (who reigns), from whom His whole family in heaven and on earth derives its name."

_____

_____

_____

_____

_____

_____

DAY 28

Daily God, you sustain me. Because of routine, life sometimes goes by in a blur. It seems to whiz by. The repeated action of doing the same thing daily cascades in my mind and I see, as if frozen in time, the reflection of the days piled upon each other. So it is at meal time, as my wife and I give You thanks, that it hits me. You provide for us over and over. I am amazed at Your repetitive goodness and mercy. You never tire of giving and blessing us with the necessities of life. You never get bored with our mundane existence!

We see life one day at a time. You Father, see the whole continuum at a single glance. You know yesterday, today and tomorrow! You are so awesome; You have my meals ready and waiting six months down the road! I work only to provide them day to day.

I realize that not everyone on earth has been provided for like this. I am extremely grateful and am completely unworthy to have been chosen by You for this kind of care. There is not a moment that goes by or a breath I take that Your Mighty Hand is not directly involved in sustaining my life. Thank you Lord; praise Your Holy Name.

Bible reference; Notes

1. Sustain;

    PS 3:5-6 – "I lie down and sleep, I wake again, because the Lord sustains me, I will not fear..."

    PS 55:22 – "Cast your cares on the Lord and He will sustain you, He will never let the righteous fall."

    PS 68:19 – "Praise be to the Lord, to God our Savior, who daily bears our burdens."

2. Thank:

    1 Chron.16:8 – "O give thanks to the Lord, call upon His name; make known His deeds among the people."

    1 Chron. 16:34 – "O give thanks to the Lord for He is good; for His loving kindness is everlasting."

    1 Cor.15:57 – "But thanks be to God, He gives us the victory through our Lord Jesus Christ."

3. Chosen:

    Prov. 16:16 – "How much better to get wisdom than gold, to choose understanding than silver."

    John 15:18 – "...but I have chosen you out of the world. That's why the world hates you."

    1 Peter 2:9 – "But you are a chosen people, a royal priesthood, a holy nation, a people belonging to the Lord.

_____

_____

_____

_____

DAY 29

The week end is here and I am so glad to have a reprieve! If it weren't for Saturdays and a break from the grinding work, life might become unbearable.

God has provided, for me, a daily reprieve. Daily the Holy Spirit comforts me and rescues me away from the constant pressures of this world. No matter what the situation in life I always have a comforting place to hide, to rest, to revive for the next day! God hides me in the cleft of the rock. He covers me there with His hand, He gathers me as does a mother hen gathers her biddies, He covers me with His wings (pinions). I am comforted in His presence. I shall not be over whelmed, flooded. He keeps me safe above the rising waters. I am convinced that neither height nor depth nor any harm shall overcome me. Eye has not seen, ear has not heard, neither has entered into the heart of man the things that God has prepared for them who love Him. "For I shall be with you always, even unto the ends of the earth." "For God so loved the world that whosoever believes in Him shall not perish, but has eternal life." If God be for me, who can be against me? "Though I walk through the valley of the shadow of death, I shall fear no evil…" Thank you God for your protection.

Bible reference; Notes

1. Rest;
    > Lev. 23:3 –"For six days work may be done, but on the seventh day there is a Sabbath of complete rest, not to do any work."
    >
    > Matt. 11:28-29 –"Come unto me all who are weary and heavy-laden and I will give you rest…you shall find rest for your souls."
    >
    > Heb. 4:3 –"For only we who believe can enter his place of rest. As for those who didn't believe, God said, 'In my anger I made a vow – They will never enter my place of rest.'"

2. Shelter;
    > PS 32:7 –"You are my hiding place; you will protect me from trouble and surround me with songs of deliverance."
    >
    > PS 61:3-4 –"For you have been my refuge (shelter), a strong tower against my for. I long to dwell in your tent forever and take refuge in the shelter of your wings."
    >
    > PS 91:4 –"He will cover you with His feathers and under His wings you will find refuge (shelter)…you will not fear."

3. Deliverer;
    > PS 18:2 –"The Lord is my rock and my fortress and my deliverer…"
    >
    > 2 Cor. 1:10 –"And he (God) did deliver us from mortal danger. And we are confident that he will continue to deliver us."
    >
    > Col. 1:13 –"For he has rescued us from the one who rules in the kingdom of darkness, and he has brought us into the Kingdom of his dear Son."

_____

_____

_____

_____

_____

_____

DAY 30

Today was a wonderful day. We were able to spend it exactly as we wanted. The sun was out, the temperature was right. It was a day that just glorified the Lord. "Day unto day utters speech and night unto night shows glory." "The heavens declare the glory of God." This day was a perfect example of that truth.

God is so anxious to display His glory for us. Our response to His glory should be praise. I honor Him, I praise Him, and He is God and Lord. His glory is from everlasting to everlasting! There is not a moment when we can't find something to praise Him about. He is awesome and Holy, almighty and righteous.

I consider the factors in my life and I realize there is not a thing I have done to deserve any of what I witness as blessings on a daily basis. He renews His blessings day to day. There is no shortage in His love, no shortage in His blessings.

Our only response is to believe and trust in His word. He is the author of life, the lover of my soul, the provider for my body and the keeper of my eternal life! How could one ask for any more? The Peace that passes all understanding is priceless. He has given it free of charge to all who believe. Praise His Holy name!

Bible reference; Notes

1. Glory;

    PS 19:1 –"The heavens are telling of the glory of God, and their expanse is declaring the works of His hands…"

    PS 86:9 –"All the nations you have made will come and worship before you O Lord, they will bring glory to your name."

    PS 186:12 –"I will praise you O Lord my God with all my heart I will glorify your name forever."

2. Renewed;

    Rom. 12:2 –"Don't copy the behavior and customs of this world, but let God transform you into a new (renewed) person by changing the way you think."

    2 Cor. 4:16 –"That is why we never give up. Though our bodies are dying, our spirits are being renewed each day."

    Eph. 1:19 –"I pray that you will begin to understand the incredible greatness of his power (to renew) for us who believe in him."

3. Praise;

    PS 96:4 –"For great is the Lord and greatly to be praised."

    PS 150:2 –"Praise Him (God) for His mighty deeds, praise Him according to His excellent greatness."

    1 Peter 2:9 –"For you are a chosen people, a Royal Priesthood, a Holy Nation, a people belonging to God that you 'may praise Him'…"

_____

_____

_____

_____

_____

_____

DAY 31

Sunday night college class! God has blessed me there for sure. Basically this is the same group of people who have been attending since I started the courses last year. Unlike a Sunday night sermon we all participate in this class. I get to hear and see what the Lord is doing in other people's lives. I get to hear firsthand how their lives are changing. In some cases, I get to see the change that comes over one when Christ has been invited into their lives. I see stark differences in their countenance and even in their external appearance! This makes God's word real for us! I have noticed the change that takes place around me.

It is a blessing to witness such testimony and to realize that God's Word is a living, life changing power. One could hear testimonies all day long, but when one sees the change first hand it is so much more powerful.

God's Word is light, truth and living. It is more than a philosophy or belief. His Word became flesh and dwelt among us. His Word is a living being; by it we receive life and are set free from the effect of the law, which is death. His Word is life! Thank you Jesus!

Bible reference; Notes

1. New;

   <u>PS 103:2-5</u> –"Praise the Lord O my soul and forget not His benefits. They forgive your sins, heal your disease, redeem your life, crown you with love, satisfy your desires, and renew your youth…"

   <u>2 Cor. 5:17</u> –"Therefore if anyone is in Christ, he is a new creation, the old has gone, the new has come."

   <u>Eph. 4:22-24</u> –"…with regard to your former way of life…put off your old self…to be made new in the attitude of your mind…put on the new self…"

2. Light;

   <u>John 8:12</u> –"When Jesus spoke, He said,' I am the light of the world. Whoever follows me will never walk in darkness but will have the light of life.' "

   <u>John 12:36</u> –"Put your trust in the light while you have it, so you may become sons (children) of light."

   <u>1 Thes. 5:5</u> –"You are all sons (children) of the light and sons (children) of the day. We do not belong to the night or to the darkness."

3. Free;

   <u>John 8:31-32</u> –"Jesus said…abide in my word… you shall know the truth and the truth shall make you free."

   <u>Rom. 6:17-18</u> –"But thanks be to God…you were slaves of sin…became obedient…you have been set free from sin…"

   <u>Gal.5:1</u> –"It is for freedom that Christ has set us free. Stand firm then and do not let yourselves be burdened again by a yoke of slavery."

DAY 32

I have been reading in Psalms 63 for a day or two now. I see Glory for God in there, I see hope for mankind in there.

In the times that our country is in now, there is much dread, much doubt and much worry. Now I realize that we should not worry about today or tomorrow, for His word says that since He feeds the sparrows of the field daily, won't He also take care of us for whom He gave so great a price? I agree, it is true that God will take care of us. He holds us in the palm of His hand.

To me it is such a sad thing to see this wonderful country, once in a covenant relationship with God Almighty, being so wasted as to fall into third world status. We have eliminated prayer from school, the Ten Commandments from our courtrooms and allowed perversion to be protected above that of Christian expression.

It seems that the powers that be are hell-bent to change this former freedom loving , God fearing country into a humanistic, secular society. But, praise God, His love is better than life! My soul will be satisfied, my lips will praise You. My soul clings to You, Your right hand upholds me. Those who seek my life will be destroyed.

Bible reference; Notes

1. Glorify;

    PS 50:23 –"But giving thanks is a sacrifice that truly honors (glorifies) me…"

    Matt. 5:16 –"…let your good deeds shine out for all to see so that everyone will praise (glorify) your Heavenly Father."

    Rom. 15:6 –"…that with one accord you may, with one voice, glorify the God and Father of our Lord Jesus Christ."

2. Hope;

    PS 146:5 –"How blessed is he whose help is the God of Jacob, whose hope is in the Lord his God."

    Col 1:27 –"…to whom God willed to make known what is the riches of the glory of this mystery among the Gentiles, which is Christ in you, the hope of glory."

    Titus 1:2 –"…a faith and knowledge resting on the hope of eternal life…which God…promised…"

3. Satisfied;

    Matt. 10:29-31 –"Are not two sparrows sold for a penny? Yet not one of them will fall to the ground apart from your Father…the very hairs of your head are numbered…do not fear, you are of more value than many sparrows."

    PS 107:8-9 –"…give thanks to the Lord for His unfailing love and wonderful deeds for men, for He satisfies the thirsty and fills the hungry with good things."

    Rom. 4:7 –"Blessed are they whose lawless deeds have been forgiven and whose sins have been covered… whose sins the Lord will not take into account."

DAY 33

In the 64th Psalm David is asking God to hear him, to hear his prayers. He is asking for protection from his enemy, but he says "the enemy" making it sound personal, as if it were Satan, who by the way, is "the enemy."

I am so very grateful that God gives me the Grace to walk during my day and sleep during my night free from the overwhelming fear of the enemy. Jesus shed His blood for me, just as if I were the only one (human) on earth. I am surrounded by His love, protected by His faithfulness. Though I may go through trials, I am always assured of their outcome. Neither height nor depth nor principalities nor powers can overcome me, for I am safe in the hands and under the protection of the Living God.

It seems the security I have in Christ could be taken for granted. But, I never want to be guilty of that. I was purchased at a great price. I take pride in what my Savior paid for me. I am that valuable to Him that He laid down His divine life and died on the cross just to purchase me and forgive my sins, so I could be saved from eternal damnation! How could I ever repay that debt? I can't. Christ did it all for free, for me!

Bible reference; Notes

1. Hear;

    PS 30:10 –"Hear O Lord and be gracious (merciful) to me, O Lord be thou my helper."

    PS 119:149 –"Hear my voice according to thy loving-kindness; revive me O Lord according to thine ordinances."

    PS 145:19 –"He will fulfill the desire of those who fear Him; He will also hear their cry and will save them."

2. Enemy;

    PS 18:3 –"I call upon the Lord who is worthy to be praised, and I am saved from my enemies."

    PS 18:48 -"He delivers me from my enemies."

    1 Cor.15:26 –"The last enemy that will be abolished is death."

3. Purchase;

    Eph.1:14 –"The Spirit is God's guarantee that He will give us everything He promised and that He has purchased us to be His own people…"

    Eph.2:13 –"…Though you were once far away from God, now you have been brought near (purchased) to Him because of the blood of Christ."

    Acts 20:28 –"…Be sure that you feed and shepherd God's flock – His Church purchased with His own blood."

_____

_____

_____

_____

_____

_____

DAY 34

During these last few months I have allowed my mind to be filled with concerns of the condition of this country, the political climate of America. Never before in history have we come so close to losing the constitutional democratic government we have today. The battle is not yet over. I constantly allow the battles going on in congress, the people's protests and the political talk shows to fill my mind and my thoughts.

We are so close to losing it! Thank God I have someone to whom I can turn. I have a Peace that passes all understanding. I have a Savior, a God that is deeply concerned about my worry and is deeply involved in what is going on. Right now I feel empty. Last night at church I felt empty. A sister gave a wonderful lesson that fit perfectly. "When the eyes of faith look up; the eyes of love look down." I want so much to have my emptiness filled with the Holy Spirit. I get so full of the world that it tends to push the Holy Spirit out. I thank my God that He is larger than the world. When all else changes, He remains. He is my Strength and my Redeemer, the One who doesn't change. I can count on Him! Praise the Lord.

Bible reference; Notes

1. Fill;

    Rom. 15:13 –"Now may the God of hope fill you with all joy and peace in believing that you may abound in hope by the power of the Holy Spirit."

    Acts 3:19 –"May you experience the love of Christ though it is so great you will never fully understand it. Then you will be filled with the fullness of life and power that comes from God."

    Rom. 8:37 –"In all these things we are more than conquerors through Him who loved us."

2. Everlasting;

    PS 103:17 –"But the loving kindness of the Lord is from everlasting to everlasting on those who fear (love) Him."

    John 6:40 –"For this is the will of my Father that everyone who beholds (sees) the Son and believes in Him may have eternal life…"

    Gen. 21:33 –"And Abraham planted a grove in Beer-Sheba and called there on the name of the Lord, the everlasting God." (El Olam)

3. Trust;

    PS 7:1 –"O Lord my God in thee do I put my trust, save me from all those who persecute me, and deliver me."

    2 Cor. 1:9-10 –"But we had the sentence of death in ourselves, that we should not trust in ourselves, but in God who raises the dead…in whom we trust that He will yet deliver us."

    1 Tim. 6:17 –"Tell those who are rich in this world not to be proud and not to trust in their money… but their trust should be in the living God…"

Kenneth L. Canion

_____

_____

_____

_____

_____

_____

DAY 35

Because God is so faithful in His continued and consistent care for us, sometimes we may have the tendency to take the state of blessedness that we are in for granted.

We get up in the morning, expecting to get up. We bathe, prepare our food, dress and drive off for work like that is the normal, anticipated thing to do. In pure numbers, I wonder how many people in the world can expect that, expect that their country is stable enough for them to be able to assume routine, repetitive tasks and be assured that their economy is strong enough to have food readily available at home or in the stores, as well as the other marketing products and services that we experience daily in our economy at this point in time. Along with that we normally are able to purchase fuel, procure mechanical services, commute to and from work on safe and efficient highways and as well be able to park in secure locations.

We naturally assume we will have lucrative employment, with time off and some benefits. We depend with confidence upon our postal system, electronic banking, interstate commerce, public education and a Department of Public Safety. All of these things we gladly pay taxes for. Our money is safe / was safe in the hands of our government. We can write checks, use debit cards, transact business electronically with great efficiency and all without too much worry. It is not just our wisdom that gave us a strong infrastructure a prospering nation. God has blessed us mightily because of the covenant relationship our forefathers established with Him. God blesses us daily! Praise His Holy Name.

Bible reference; Notes

1. Faithful;

Deu.7:9 – "Know therefore that the Lord your God, He is God the faithful God who keeps His covenant and His loving kindness to a thousand generations with those who love Him and keep His commandments."

1 Cor. 1:9 – "God is faithful through whom you were called into fellowship with His son, Jesus Christ our Lord."

2 Thes.3:3 – "But the Lord is faithful and He will strengthen and protect you from the evil one."

2. Blessing;

Neh. 9:5 – "…Arise, bless the Lord your God forever and ever, O may thy glorious name be blessed and exalted above all blessings and praise. (6) Thou alone are the Lord."

PS 5:12 – "For you bless the godly O Lord, surrounding them with your shield of love."

Heb. 6:13 – "For when God made the promise to Abraham…He swore by Himself…I will surely bless you, I will surely multiply you."

3. Benefits;

PS 68:19 – "Blessed be the Lord who daily bears our burden. The God who is our salvation."

PS 103:2 – "Praise the Lord, I tell myself, and never forget the good things he does for me."

2 Chron. 32:25 – "But Hezekiah did not respond appropriately for the benefit he received and became proud, so the Lord's anger came against him…"

_____

_____

_____

_____

_____

_____

DAY 36

Every day, O Lord is filled with your Glory and Grace. Daily I struggle to walk in the "Light". Daily I fail to remain in His presence. I know now why God gave the Law. Its purpose was to show that we cannot gain righteousness by our own struggle. Praise be. God is there each morning to renew our strength and forgive our confessed sin that we may start fresh each morning.

His Grace is sufficient for all our sin. He is our source of renewal. Without Him all things would be lost. Thank you Jesus for your outstanding plan that takes me out of the miry pit and puts me next to you on high with the Father.

Your plan is perfect. Jesus paid the price for all my sin, past, present and future. The Holy Spirit lives within me, gently leading me along righteous paths. The Father set it all up and is waiting for my time on earth to be over so he can reward me with life eternal! What a great glory that is! The perfection of this plan of salvation by our Creator is perfect! No matter what my condition, position or station in life, he is always there just waiting to do good things for me! It can't get any better than that!

Bible reference; Notes

1. Fill;

    Matt. 5:6 –"God blesses those who are hungry and thirsty for justice for they will receive it in full."(Shall be filled)

    Acts 2:4 –"and everyone present was filled with the Holy spirit and began speaking in other languages as the Holy Spirit gave them the ability."

    PS 23:5-6 –"…my cup overflows with blessings. Surely your goodness and unfailing love will pursue me all the days of my life."

2. Renew;

    Isa. 40:31 –"Yet those who wait for the Lord will gain new (renew) their strength. They will mount up with wings like eagles. They will run and not get tired; they will walk and not become weary."

    Rom. 12:2 –"and do not be conformed to this world but be transformed by the renewing of your mind that you may prove what the will of God is that which is good and acceptable and perfect."

    Eph. 4:22-23 –"…lay- aside the old self which is being corrupted…that you be renewed in the spirit of your mind."

3. Forgive;

    Matt. 6:14 –"If you forgive those who sin against you, your Heavenly Father will forgive you."

    Col. 3:13 –"You must make allowances for each other's faults and forgive the person who offends you…the Lord forgave you, so you must forgive others."

    Eph. 4:32 –"Instead be kind to each other, tenderhearted, forgiving one another, just as God through Christ has forgiven you."

Kenneth L. Canion

_____

_____

_____

_____

_____

_____

DAY 37

God is good, all the time. Today was the first day off from school, the beginning of Spring break. I spent the day in the house, most of it in bed. My mind and body were tired and sick. My chest congestion and coughing got the best of me, so I just rested up to be renewed in strength.

God renews me in spirit daily. The cares and activities of the day weigh me down each evening. My spirit becomes heavy, but God is faithful to never leave me and He gladly lifts the burdens of my soul each day. I don't have to carry the worries of the day with me. It is His job to restore life and He serves to make me glad in Him.

There is no way I could face the world daily without the Holy Spirit to strengthen me when I am well, much less than when I am physically ill. The burden would be too much to bear. But God is faithful and just and will not allow me to be burdened with more than I can bear. He does, with each burden, provide a way of escape, that I may be able to stand it all. It is in the comfort of the presence of the Holy Spirit, on a daily basis, that I rejoice.

Bible reference; Notes

1. Rest;

   <u>PS 37:7</u> –"Rest in the Lord and wait patiently for Him; fret not thyself…"

   <u>Matt.11:28-29</u> –"Jesus said, come to me all of you who are weary and carry heavy burdens and I will give you rest. Take my yoke upon you. Let me teach you, because I am humble and gentle and you will find rest for your souls."

   <u>Heb. 4:3-4</u> –"For only we who believe can enter His place of rest. As for those who do not believe, God said, they will never enter my place of rest."

2. Thirst;

   <u>PS 42:1</u> –"As the deer pants for streams of water, so I long for you O God. I thirst for God, the Living God."

   <u>John 4:10</u> –"Jesus replied…you would ask me and I would give you living water."

   <u>John 4:13</u> –"But, the water I give them takes away thirst altogether."

3. Burden;

   <u>PS 55:22</u> –"Give your burdens to the Lord and He will take care of you."

   <u>Matt. 11:30</u> –"For my yoke fits perfectly and the burden I give you is light."

   <u>Gal. 6:2</u> –"Bear ye one another's burdens and so fulfill the law of Christ."

_____

_____

_____

_____

DAY 38

This was a good day. I was blessed by the Lord all day long. It was Sunday and we skipped church to prepare and leave for some camping at Moss Hill. Praise God, we have been freed from the law. There is no condemnation on missing a worship gathering now and again. My God is not an ogre sitting on a throne waiting to bonk people on the head. Jesus, my Christ, fulfilled all parts of the law. He took upon Himself the sins in my life and suffered the penalty of the law for me! What greater joy can a person have than to realize eternal life is theirs through belief in the Son of God!

My son and family joined us at the deer camp for the day. What joy there is in seeing one's grandchildren and to observe the growth taking place in them. His family is solid, everything looks good. They even went to church before coming out today. All this joy is in the natural. I can't imagine what awaits us when He claims His own and we are in eternity. "Eye has not seen, nor has ear heard, neither has entered into the heart of man the things that God has prepared for them who love Him! How great it is!

Bible reference; Notes

1. Free;

    John 8:32 –"…and you will know the truth and the truth will set you free."

    Rom. 6:22 –"But not you are free from the power of sin…now you do those things that lead to holiness and eternal life. For the wages of sin is death, but the free gift of God is eternal life through Jesus Christ our Lord."

    Gal. 5:1 –"So Christ has really set us free. Now make sure that you stay free and don't get tied up again in slavery to the law."

2. Condemnation;

    John 5:24 –"I assure you, those who listen…and believe in God who sent me, have eternal life. They will never be condemned…but have already passed from death into life."

    Rom. 8:1 –"So now, there is no condemnation for those who belong to Christ Jesus."

    2 Cor. 3:9 –"If the old covenant, which brings condemnation was glorious, how much more glorious is the New Covenant which makes us right with God."

3. Joy;

    Luke 15:7 –"I tell you…there will be more joy in heaven over one sinner who repents, than over ninety-nine righteous persons who need no repentance."

    John 15:10-11 –"If you keep my commandments you will abide in my love…These things I have spoken to you that my joy may be in you and that your joy may be made full."

John 16:24 –"You haven't done this before. Ask, using my name, and you will receive, and you will have abundant joy."

_____

_____

_____

_____

_____

_____

DAY 39

In the woods; we are in the woods. Everyone has gone home. My wife and I are here enjoying the serenity of God's perfect creation. The Holy Spirit abides with us. He, The Comforter, gives us the peace that passes all understanding.

When I think of the value, the beauty, of what I am experiencing now, it seems priceless, and in fact is priceless. Money can't buy that peace, knowledge can't secure it, only the presence of the Comforter can provide it. It didn't cost me a thing. This peace we have is far greater and far more expensive than the most exclusive get-away island in the world. Jesus paid it all, He paid the price for me. All I had to do to receive it was to believe and obey. It really goes deeper than that, though. He called my name before I was born. He chose me out of the tangled mass, I was but a worm, and He declared me worthy. He calls those who will believe the same way.

How can one overlook such a gift as that? How can anything on earth make one get depressed, when there is so much joy that my Savior has provided? There are times I will get down, but praise God, He is always there, willing to bear me up again to receive His joy!

Bible reference; Notes

1. Beauty;

    <u>PS 8:1</u> –"O Lord our Lord, how majestic is thy name in all the earth, who has displayed thy splendor above the heavens."

    <u>PS 19:1</u> –"The heavens declare the glory of God and the firmament shows His handiwork."

    <u>PS 27:4</u> –"One thing I have asked from the Lord that I shall seek; That I may dwell in the house of the Lord all the days of my life to behold the beauty of the Lord…"

2. Comfort;

    <u>John 14:16</u> –"And I will ask the Father and He will give you another helper (comforter) that He may be with you "

    <u>John 14:26</u> –"But the Comforter, who is the Holy Spirit, whom the Father will send in my name, He shall teach you all things and bring all things to your remembrance, whatever I have said unto you."

    <u>2 Cor.1:3</u> –"All praise to the God and Father of our Lord Jesus Christ. He is the source of every mercy and the God who comforts us."

3. Peace;

    <u>John 14:27</u> –"I am leaving you with a gift – peace of mind and heart. And the peace I give isn't like the peace the world gives."

    <u>Rom. 5:1</u> –"therefore since we have been made right in God's sight by faith, we have peace with God because of what Jesus Christ our Lord has done for us."

    <u>Phil. 4:7</u> –"And the Peace of God, which surpasses all understanding (comprehension) shall guard your heart and your mind in Christ Jesus."

DAY 40

God is great! He does not overlook the smallest detail of our need, not want, need. We are enjoying His nature in the woods. No one is here, just us and the Holy Spirit. Today was a down day; it drizzled and rained all day long. I find in the most mundane circumstance that God provides for us, even if we are not aware.

This camping place is eight long miles deep in the East Texas woods, down a long unpaved logging road. The water supply, normally good, was out because of the earlier freezes that caused the pipes to burst. Instead of complaining about the rainy day we just relaxed and enjoyed it. The next morning we had collected ample water to provide for all of our needs! Where in God's word does it say he will provide water for toilet flushing needs? His word says He cares for us and will provide for all our needs. Well, that was just proven true.

God, you are so good! I thank you so much for supplying all our needs. In fact, Lord, I thank you for my needs. It is great to see your hand at work in fulfilling them in my life. How great it is to be in the hands of a living God. How fearful I would be if I were not in His hands.

Bible reference; Notes

1. Magnified;
   <u>1 Chron. 17:23-24</u> –"And now Lord, let the word that you have spoken concerning your servant and…his house be established forever, and do as you have spoken and let your name be established and magnified forever…"

   <u>PS 35:27</u> –"Let them shout for joy and be glad who favor my righteous cause. Yes, let them say continuously, 'Let the Lord be magnified…'

   <u>Luke 1:46-47</u> –"And Mary said, 'My soul doth magnify the Lord, and my spirit hath rejoiced in God my Savior."

2. Presence;
   <u>1 Chron. 16:27</u> –"Glory and honor are in His presence; strength and gladness are in His place."

   <u>1 Chron. 16:33</u> –"Then shall the trees of the woods sing out at the presence of the Lord, because He comes to judge the earth."

   <u>PS 95:2</u> –"Let us come before His presence with thanksgiving. Let us shout joyfully to Him…"

3. Need;
   <u>Phil. 4:19</u> –"And my God shall supply all your needs according to His riches in glory in Christ Jesus."

   <u>Heb. 4:16</u> –"Let us therefore draw near with confidence to the Throne of Grace, that we may receive mercy and may find grace to help in time of need."

   <u>Rev. 22:5</u> –"and there shall no longer be any night, and they shall not have need of the light of a lamp or the…sun because the Lord God shall illumine them forever…"

_____

_____

_____

_____

_____

_____

DAY 41

Here I sit in God's beautiful sunlight. He has provided for us another blessed day. I experience such freedom and abundance when my wife and I are in the woods. Everything is quiet, only the sound of nature is heard. When all the trappings of society are removed, when there is no input to your senses except what God has provided in nature, the world takes on a different view. No longer does one question what is right or wrong. There is no distraction planned by the evil one that will confound or confuse your thinking.

I think that is why God showed Himself in the "still small voice" to Elijah after the storm, the earthquake and the thunder. God is after our innermost self. He reveals Himself through the Holy Spirit when we have stripped all the veneer away and truly become alone with Him.

It is a wonderful thing to be in the hands of a living God. I am so grateful and truly blessed because of His care for me. Here is another blessing to remember. Satan, the evil one, is a created being just like me. As my days on this earth are numbered, so are his. He is limited. God is not. Whom shall I fear?

Bible reference; Notes

1. Sun;

> <u>Deut. 4:19</u> –"And when you look up into the sky and see the sun - all the forces of heaven – don't be seduced by them and worship them."
>
> <u>PS 74:16</u> –"O God…Both day and night belong to you, you made the starlight and the sun."
>
> <u>Matt. 5:45</u> –"…your Father in Heaven. For He gives His sunlight to both the evil and the good, and He sends rain on the just and unjust…"

2. Sound;

> <u>PS 89:15-16</u> –"How blessed are the people who know the joyful sound! O Lord, they walk in the light of Thy countenance. In Thy name they rejoice all the day…"
>
> <u>Rom. 10:18</u> –"But I say, have they not heard? (God's Word) Yes, verily, their sound went into all the earth and their words unto the ends of the world."
>
> <u>1 Thes. 1:8</u> –"And now the Word of the Lord is ringing out (sounding out) from you to people everywhere…"

3. Evil;

> <u>Gen. 6:5</u> –"Now the Lord observed the extent of the people's wickedness, and He saw that all their thoughts were consistently and totally evil."
>
> <u>2 Chron. 33:22</u> –"And he did what was evil in the Lord's sight…He worshipped and sacrificed to all the idols…"
>
> <u>PS 34:16</u> –"But the Lord turns His face against those who do evil; He will erase their memory form the earth."

_____

_____

_____

_____

_____

DAY 42

This day is wonderful in my eyes. It only attests to the Glory of what is to come. God in His perfection gives to everyone His blessings. The rain falls on the just and the unjust. I think perhaps the only difference in the just and the unjust receiving His blessings is the fact that His Glory is recognized by one and not the other. A gift is not a gift unless it is perceived as a gift. Those who have their spiritual eyes open see our daily provisions as a special gift from God. Those who are blind spiritually see each day as just another "happenstance" that occurs because of the climate, natural conditions or some phenomenon in nature. (Now we see through a glass darkly, but then we shall see face to face.) In other words, when the Holy Spirit enters in, we get a whole new set of eyes.

Even at its best, this day cannot begin to compare to what God has prepared for them who love Him. His miracles never cease, it is just our eyes that either grow dim or are opened by the amount of freedom we give to the Holy Spirit in our life. He gives us freedom.

Bible references; Notes

1. Day:

   John 6:40 –"For this is the will of my Father, that everyone who beholds the Son and believes in Him may have eternal life, and I myself will raise him up on the last day."

   John 8:56 –"Your father Abraham rejoiced to see my day, and he saw it and was glad."

   John 9:4 –"We must work the works of Him who sent me, as long as it is day; night is coming when no man can work."

2. Perfect;

   PS 18:30 –"As for God, His way is perfect. All the Lord's promises prove true."

   1 John 4:17 –"And as we live in God, our love grows more perfect so we will not be afraid on the day of judgment, but we can face Him with confidence because we are like Christ here in this world."

   1 John 2:5 –"…but whosoever keeps His word, in him the love of God has truly been perfected. By this we know that we are in Him."

3. Unjust;

   Prov. 29:27 –"An unjust man is an abomination to the just; and he that is upright in the way is an abomination to the wicked."

   Mat.5:44-45 –"but I say love your enemies…In that way you will be acting as true children of your Father in Heaven. For He…sends rain on the just and on the unjust too.

   Acts 24:15 –"…have hope toward God…there shall be a resurrection of the dead, both of the just and unjust."

———————————————————————

———————————————————————

———————————————————————

———————————————————————

———————————————————————

———————————————————————

DAY 43

"Then sings my soul, my savior God to thee, how great thou are, how great you are." Lord God, you are great and awesome, holy and perfect. You lay the course for each life; your plan for us is a future, not calamity. When we miss your path, we fall short of the Glory of God. You are saddened when we fall so short. Your wish for us is glorious.

I see the hurt and anxiety of others over the life choices their children have made. I witness the stories of heartbreak and see the despair on the face of the parents and hear it in their voice as they describe the convoluted mess their children get themselves into. It saddens me just listening. I can only imagine what it does to you, Lord. They talk of doctors, medicine, psychiatrists and so forth. The simple and plain answer is Jesus Christ, through the power of the Holy Spirit.

God, my Father, I am eternally grateful for what you have done with my children. I can take no credit for their outcome. You and you alone, Lord, are our Savior and our salvation. You have filled me with the peace that passes all understanding and have surely blessed my children with stable lives. Thank you so much. I pray Lord; they will learn to stand closer to you, to give you the attention you deserve.

Bible reference; Notes

1. Sing;

    PS 13:6 –"I will sing unto the Lord because He has been so good to me."

    1 Cor. 14:15 –"Well then, what shall I do? I will do both…I will sing in the Spirit and I will sing in words I understand."

    Jas. 5:13 –"Are any among you suffering? They should keep on praying about it. And those who have reason to be thankful should continually sing praise to the Lord."

2. Hope;

    Jer. 29:11 –"For I know the plans that I have for you, declares the Lord, plans for welfare and not calamity to give you a future and a hope."

    PS 31:24 –"Be strong and let your heart take courage, all you who hope in the Lord."

    Rom. 15:13 –"So I pray that God who gives you hope will keep you happy and full of peace…May you overflow with hope through the power of the Holy Spirit."

3. Children;

    Matt.19:14 –"Jesus said, Let the children come unto me, don't stop them, for the Kingdom of Heaven belongs to such as these."

    Eph. 6:1 –"Children, obey your parents in the Lord, for this is right."

    Eph. 6:4 –"And fathers, do not provoke your children to anger, but bring them up in the discipline and instruction of the Lord."

DAY 44

People always have the tendency to take things for granted, to believe things will always stay the same. We assumed we would make our way home successfully in the rain yesterday. We assumed that every mechanical aspect of our trip, pulling the trailer in the rain, would continue to function as designed, especially on such a day with terrible weather conditions. Our assumptions were not based on the soundness of the mechanical devises we have, but on the reliance upon the guidance and blessings of God through the Holy Spirit.

I have to give God the credit for success of a trip in such terrible conditions and such stress on the equipment. Our prayer and the plea for "travel mercies" plus the expectations of God's blessings on our daily activities are the reason the trip came off without a hitch. I can't even imagine the number of individual events, possible calamities that God knows about in each of our lives. Things like timing at intersections, strength of hydraulic lines, debris scattered on the road, animal crossings, slick spots, wind gusts, driver fatigue, tire performance or a myriad of other circumstances could serve to alter one's life on earth.

We humans are so fragile. But, God's Word is so great! How blessed we are to have the Creator of this universe care enough for us individually to know and care about every aspect of our lives!

Bible reference; Notes

1. Expect;

     Luke 4:25 –"…woman said, I know (expect) the Messiah is coming (He who is called Christ); when that One comes He will declare all things to us."

     Phil. 4:19 –"And my God shall supply all your needs according to His riches in Glory in Christ Jesus."

     Heb. 13:8 –"Jesus Christ is the same yesterday, today, yes and forever."

2. Bless;

     PS 24:5 –"The earth is the Lords and everything in it. The world and all its people belong to Him. They will receive the Lord's blessing and have right standing with God their Savior."

     Eph. 1:3 –"How we praise God, the Father of our Lord Jesus Christ, who has blessed us with every spiritual blessing…because we belong to Christ."

     Heb. 6:14 –"I will certainly bless you richly…"

3. Know;

     PS 9:10 –"And those who know Thy name will put their trust in Thee, for Thou O Lord has not forsaken those who seek Thee.

     PS 46:10 –"Cease striving and know that I am God…"

     Matt. 7:11 –"If you then, being evil, know how to give good gifts to your children, how much more shall your Father who is in heaven give what is good to those who ask Him?"

DAY 45

Lord, I see your blessings in my life even more when I see and hear the trials in the lives of my Christian brothers and sisters. You give me a perspective in my life. It strikes fear into my heart when I see what others are going through. To me, they become walking heroes. They are evidence of putting on the whole armor of God.

I am confident that You are faithful and just and will not allow them to be tempted more than they are able to bear, but will with that temptation, trial, provide a way of escape for them. This victory-overcoming- is provided for in Your Word, of that I am confident. I thank you Lord for your provisions for us as we struggle through life here on earth.

We know and are sure of the fact that there will always be a brighter day. Our trust in you is never wasted and is always rewarded. For if God so loved the world that He gave His only begotten son. How could we not know that He has reserved for us a place greater that all our imagination could ever conjure? God is good all the time. I am so thankful that His grace and mercy far outweigh my feeble attempt to live the life of a Christian. God, you have mercy on me, and I thank you for it.

Bible reference; Notes

1. Trial;

    1 Peter 4:12 –"…don't be surprised at the fiery trials you are going through, as if something strange were happening to you…be very glad because these trials will make you partners with Christ in His suffering."

2. Evidence;

    Heb. 11:1 –"…faith? It is the confident assurance that what we hope for is going to happen. It is the evidence of things we cannot yet see."

3. Armor;

    Eph. 6:11 –"Put on all of God's armor so that you will be able to stand firm against all the strategies and tricks of the Devil. For we are not fighting against people made of flesh and blood, but against the evil rulers and authorities of the unseen world, against those mighty powers of darkness who rule this world and against wicked spirits in the heavenly realms."

4. Faithful;

    1 Cor. 10:13 –"There hath no temptation taken you but such as is common to man; but God is faithful who will not permit you to be tempted above that ye are able; but will with the temptation also make the way to escape that ye may be able to bear it."

5. Hope;

    Jer. 17:7 –"Blessed are those who trust in the Lord and have made the Lord their hope and confidence."

    John 3:16-17 –"For God so loved the world that He gave His only son so that everyone who believes in Him will not perish but have eternal life. God did not send His Son into the world to condemn it, but to save it."

_____

_____

_____

_____

_____

_____

DAY 46

Expectation: This day was the first day back to work after Spring Break. During my time off I held an expectation to return to work, an expectation to be paid for my efforts, an expectation to continue to live in the manner in which I am accustomed. This expectation was dependent upon the conventions of man. They were met, with little thought to the contrary. This was and is a blessing to me and to the millions who continue their lives daily. Because it is of man there is always a possibility that those expectations will not be met. Any number of reasons could prevent it. War, famine, collapse, death are just a few of the factors that could prevent those expectations form being met.

However, my expectations of God are a sure thing. In these I am blessed also, and in these I live and look forward to their fulfillment. There is absolutely no chance of my expectations in God not being met. (John 1:1) –"In the beginning was the Word and the Word was with God and the Word was God." (Heb. 1:1) –"God …in these last days spoke to us…His Son…by whom He made the worlds… upholding all things by the Word of His power…" (1John 1:1) –"that which was from the beginning…and declare unto you that eternal life…was manifest unto us…" These are three witnesses that guarantee my expectations of God!

Bible reference; Notes

1. Hope;

   PS 16:8 –"I know the Lord is always with me, I will not be shaken, for He is right beside me."

   PS 31:23 –"Love the Lord, all you faithful ones. For the Lord protects those who are loyal to Him."

   Jer. 17:7 –"But blessed are those who trust in the Lord and have made the Lord their hope and confidence."

2. Expectation;

   PS 62:5 –"I wait quietly before God for my expectation is in Him."

   Prov. 10:28 –"The hopes of the godly result in happiness, but the expectations of the wicked are all in vain."

   Jer. 29:11 –"For I know the plans I have for you, says the Lord. They are plans for good and not for disaster, to give you a future and a hope."

3. Witness;

   John 5:36 (Jesus talking) –"but I have a greater witness than John – my teachings and my miracles. They have been assigned to me by my Father and they testify (witness) that the Father has sent me."

   John 5:37 –"And the Father himself also has testified about me."

   John 5:39 –"You search the scriptures because you believe they give you eternal life, but the scriptures point to me. Yet you refuse to come to me so that I can give you this eternal life."

Kenneth L. Canion

_____

_____

_____

_____

DAY 47

The King is coming! Praise God He is coming for me! A day is just any day; they fall by the wayside one after the other. Home to work, work to home. One could get lost in the repetition of life. Repeated daily events have a way of reducing themselves into mundane, automatic repetition of motion, almost ending up in meaningless existence.

However, for those who love the Lord and are called to His purpose, life takes on a new meaning. Every moment is a reward, whether recognized as such or not. The relationship God has provided for those who love Him can never grow stale or stagnant. God has given each one of us a peaceful present and future. We don't have to worry about what tomorrow will bring. We no longer live in fear or slavery to the law (of sin and death). Those who love Him are free, free indeed. We are free to enjoy the day, the moment.

Joy and happiness are what He has given us. We know that each day that passes is one day closer to being in His presence. We know that we are being prepared to serve in the Kingdom. We are being groomed for our new jobs, so to speak. He has plans for us; we have a future. He provides this for us on a daily basis. Thank you Lord!

Bible reference; Notes

1. King;

    <u>1 Tim. 1:17</u> – "Now unto the King eternal, immortal, invincible, the only wise God, be honor and glory for ever and ever. Amen."

    <u>1 Tim. 6:15</u> – "For at the right time, Christ will be revealed from Heaven by the blessed and only Almighty God, the King of kings and Lord of lords."

    <u>Rev. 15:3</u> – "And they were singing the song of Moses, the servant of God, and the song of the Lamb: Great and marvelous are your actions Lord God Almighty. Just and true are your ways O' King of the nations."

2. Free;

    <u>Rom. 5:15</u> – "…what a difference between our sin and God's generous (free) gift of forgiveness."

    <u>Rom. 5:18</u> – "… Adam's one sin brought condemnation upon everyone, but Christ's (free) act of righteousness makes all people right in God's sight and gives them life."

    <u>Rom. 6:18</u> – "Now you are free from sin, your old master, and you have become slaves to your new master, righteousness."

3. Purpose;

    <u>Rom. 8:28</u> – "…we know that God causes everything to work together for the good of those who love God and are called according to His purpose."

    <u>Eph. 3:11</u> – "this was His plan from all eternity, and it has now been carried out through Jesus Christ our Lord."

    <u>2 Tim. 1:9</u> – "It is God who saves us and chose us to live a Holy life. He did this not because we deserve it, but because that was His plan (purpose) long before the world began…"

DAY 48

I am dry Lord. My spirit seems to have retreated from you. The joy is there, but my heart is not rejoicing in you. I really hate it when these times come upon me. I don't really know the cause, but I imagine that the reason is me. I have moved out from under the Light. The assurance I have in this is that I know my God. The Creator of the Universe cannot lie. He has said in His Word that He will never leave or forsake me. He sent the Holy Spirit to live within me. The Holy Spirit is not fickle and does not leave me. He is a still small voice, waiting patiently for me to get my heart right again.

What greater joy can a man have than to realize that the God he serves is not dependent upon human strength or will or obedience. I am so glad my salvation is based on God's Word and not on my ability to keep His law. Thank you God, so much, for such a great gift. Thank you for the righteousness you have imputed to me through the Blood of Christ. I am so glad I can depend on you. God said it that settles it!

Bible reference; Notes

1. Dry;

    PS 51:10 –"Create in me a clean heart, O God; renew a right spirit within me."

    PS 63:1 "O God, thou art my God, early will I seek thee, my soul thirsteth for thee, my flesh longeth for thee in a dry and thirsty land where no water is."

    PS 68:6 –"God makes a home for the lonely; He leads out the prisoners into prosperity. Only the rebellious dwell in a parched (dry) land."

2. Spirit;

    PS 51:11-12 –"Do not banish me from your presence, and don't take your Holy Spirit from me. Restore to me again the joy of your salvation."

    PS 77:3 –"I think of God and I moan, overwhelmed with longing for His help (Spirit)."

    PS 139:7 –"I can never escape from your Spirit; I can never get away from your presence."

3. Reprieve;

    PS 27:1 –"The Lord is my light and my salvation – so why should I be afraid?"

    John 12:46 –"I have come as a light to shine in this dark world, so that all who put their trust in me will no longer remain in the darkness."

    James 2:24 –"We are made right with God by what we do, not by faith alone."

_____

_____

_____

DAY 49

I can't get this song out of my head. "All night, all day, someone's looking after me..." That is my joy today. Someone is looking after me! When my eyes are opened by faith that becomes apparent. Sometimes I close my eyes to the Spirit. It is during those times that I feel dry and alone.

The great disappointment in my life is that I cannot always remain "fully charged", so to speak. I allow things, fatigue or negative influences to dim my spiritual eyes. There is a difference between an intellectual ascent to the Holy Spirit and truly "being in the Spirit." If I could, while here on earth, I would remain in the Spirit continually. But, I cannot. One day, in Heaven, we will be in His presence continually. Right now I'll just have to know my human weakness doesn't allow that to happen.

The comfort in it is that His Word is true, regardless what man thinks. In the end all things in existence will be changed, His word will not. All things will be cast away, His Word will remain. So, regardless of what I think or feel, His Word is constant and that is what I can base my happiness on!

Bible reference; Notes

1. Eyes;

>PS 17:8 –"O Lord…guard me as the apple of your eye. Hide me in the shadow of your wings."
>
>PS 32:8 –"The Lord says; 'I will guide you along the best paths for your life. I will advise you and watch over you. (I will guide thee with mine eye.)'"
>
>2 Chron. 16:9 –"The eyes of the Lord search the whole earth in order to strengthen those whose hearts are fully committed to Him."

2. Faith;

>Matt. 6:30 –"And if God cares so wonderfully for flowers that are here today and gone tomorrow, won't he more surely care for you? You have such little faith."
>
>Matt. 9:22 –"Jesus turned and said to her, 'Daughter be encouraged, your faith has made you well (whole)."
>
>Acts 20:21 –"–"(Paul speaking) –"I have had one message for Jews and Gentiles alike – the necessity of turning from sin and turning to God and of faith in our Lord Jesus Christ."

3. Change;

>Mal. 3:6 –"I am the Lord, and I do not change."
>
>Phil. 3:21 –"He will take these weak mortal bodies of ours and change them into glorious bodies like His own, using the same mighty power that He will use to conquer everything, everywhere."
>
>1 Cor. 15:51 –"But let me tell you a wonderful secret God has revealed to us. Not all of us will die, but we will be transformed (Changed)."

DAY 50

I surrender, I surrender all, is the song that keeps going through my mind. When you think about it, there is comfort in that thought. Yesterday was Friday, the last day of the work-week. With Friday comes the pressures of the week to a culmination. In my job, the students, as normal, are certainly not cooperative. My body is tired, my mind is tired and all I can think about is getting the day over and taking a break.

Yet, in the midst of all the turmoil, the promise of God remains. His strength, His peace, His comfort, His Holy Spirit are there to comfort me. Surrendering to the Will of God in the midst of such pressure and confusion is a great source of joy. I can't see living a life, any longer, outside of the veil of God's Love. I am so thankful that I do not have to face life here on earth on my own strength. Living outside of God's provisions would be so scary, so depressing I would really be a basket case.

When I think about the times I rejected the Holy Spirit in my life, it scares me. He is my protection, my escape route, my guaranteed ticket to eternal life in His presence. I have a song in my heart.

Bible reference; Notes

1. Rest;

    Isa. 28:12 –"God's people could have rest in their own land, if they would only obey Him, but they will not listen."

    Isa. 30:15 –"For thus the Lord God, the Holy One of Israel, has said 'In repentance and rest you shall be saved. In quietness and trust is your strength."

    Matt.11:28 –"Then Jesus said, 'Come to me all you who are weary and carry heavy burdens and I will give you rest."

2. Promise;

    Luke 24:49 –"And now I will send the Holy Spirit, just as my Father promised. But stay here…until the Holy Spirit comes and fills you with power from Heaven."

    Acts 2:33 –"Now He sits on His throne of highest honor in Heaven at God's right hand. And the Father, as He promised, gave Him the Holy Spirit to pour out upon us, just as you see and hear today."

    Gal 3:14 –"Through the work of Christ Jesus, God has blessed the Gentiles with the same blessings He promised to Abraham, and we Christians receive the promised Holy Spirit through faith."

3. Strength;

    1 Chron. 16:11 –"Search for the Lord and for His strength and keep on searching."

    PS 18:32 –"God arms me with strength; He has made my way safe."

    Mk. 12:30 –"(Jesus speaking) –"And you must love the Lord your God with all your heart, all your soul, all your mind and all your strength."

_____

_____

_____

_____

DAY 51

"It's me, it's me, it's me O Lord, standing in the need of prayer..." I awoke this morning with that song running through my head. I am so thankful that the Lord puts a song in my heart. He makes my soul merry. He restores my soul; He leads me beside the still waters. He guides me in the paths of righteousness. Even though I walk through the "Valley of Death" I don't need to fear. He covers me like a hen covers her biddies with her wings. He hides me in the cleft of the rock and covers me there with His hands. What have I to fear from mere man who can only kill the body? My God gives life to the body and the spirit. My God is real; His glory is from everlasting unto everlasting. He sees everything that happens to me and He desires a future for me.

Glory! No matter what befall us, God can conquer all things. We are secure in His arms. There is no greater joy to be had on this earth than that of being in the arms of our loving God whom we wake up to daily. It is not just one thing the Lord has done for us, it is everything. We know we fight not against flesh and blood, but against principalities and powers. God's got our back. We are safe and secure!

Bible reference; Notes

1. Stand;

    <u>Isa. 40:8</u> –"The grass withers and the flowers fade, but the Word of our God stands forever."

    <u>Rom. 14:10</u> –"…Remember, each of us will stand personally before the judgment seat of God…every knee will bow …every tongue will confess (that Jesus Christ is Lord.)."

    <u>Eph. 6:11</u> –"Put on the whole armor of God so that you will be able to stand firm against all the strategies and tricks of the devil."

2. Need;

    <u>Matt. 6:32</u> –"Why be like the pagans…your Heavenly Father already knows all your needs and He will give all you need from day to day if you live for Him…"

    <u>Phil. 4:19</u> –"And this same God who takes care of me (Paul) will supply all your needs from His glorious riches, which have been given to us in Christ Jesus."

    <u>Heb. 4:16</u> –"So, let us come boldly to the throne of our gracious God. There we will receive His mercy and we will find grace to help us (in time of need)."

3. Rock;

    <u>PS 18:2</u> –"The Lord is my rock, my fortress and my savior."

    <u>Matt. 7:24</u> – (Jesus talking) "Anyone who listens to my teachings and obeys me is wise, like a person who builds a house upon a solid rock."

    <u>1 Cor. 10:14</u> –"…For they all drank from that same miraculous rock that traveled with them, and that rock was Christ."

_____

_____

_____

_____

_____

DAY 52

God, I am thankful for the Christian family you have provided for me. You do good things for me daily. Being planted in the midst of this church family has blessed me with much growth in Christ and I am thankful. I have learned that as a Christian one must be involved with others. The prayer, the sharing and the testimonies of others add richness to my experience in Christ that I could not obtain by being a believer separate from a body in Christ.

To me this is a phenomenon that occurs only when you actually involve yourself in others' lives. In some mysterious way, when other people receive a blessing or a break through, it affects those who witness it. I know the change I have gone through. I can compare my attitude before I was surrounded by these believers and since I have been surrounded by them. A change has occurred that would not have been possible if I had not involved myself in the college classes and the group meetings we now have. This is growth, Christian growth for me. I am thankful for it. My wife and I have both grown closer to the Holy Spirit

Bible reference; Notes

1. Family;

    <u>Deu.29:18</u> –"the Lord made this (His) covenant with you so that no man, woman, family, tribe among you would turn away from the Lord our God…"

    <u>Jer. 10:25</u> –"Pour out your wrath on the nations that refuse to recognize you, on nations (families) that do not call upon your name."

    <u>Eph. 3:15</u> –"…I bow my knees before the Father from whom every family in heaven and on earth derives its name."

2. Christian;

    <u>Acts 11:26</u> –"…It was there at Antioch that the believers were first called Christians."

    <u>1 Cor. 4:10</u> –"We are fools for Christ's sake…" *NOB – "Our dedication to Christ makes us look like fools…" *LASB

    <u>1 Peter 4:16</u> –"For it is no shame to suffer for being a Christian. Praise God for the privilege of being called by His wonderful name."

3. Daily;

    <u>PS 68:19</u> –"Praise the Lord; praise God our Savior! For each day He carries us in His arms."

    <u>Luke 9:23</u> –"(Jesus speaking) –"If any of you wants to be my follower you must put aside your selfish ambition, shoulder your cross daily and follow me."

    <u>Heb. 3:13</u> –"but encourage one another day after day (daily) as long as it is still called today so that none of you will be deceived by sin and hardened against God."

*NOB –New Open Bible, *LASB –Life Application Study Bible

_____

_____

_____

_____

_____

_____

DAY 53

God is faithful and just. He always restores my soul. There are "dry times" in my spiritual walk. It is during these times that I seem to have moved away from the Holy Spirit. My prayer life seems empty and I lose the song in my heart. I know God has not abandoned me. The problem is that I have moved from Him. I don't like those times, but they happen. I find that I can be restored by just perusing the Word of God. Busying myself in His Word will rejoin the broken connection.

It is my nature that is at fault. The natural man in me does not desire to fellowship with the Lord. My natural desire is to fulfill the lusts of the flesh. The spirit-man in me is renewed by fellowship with the Holy Spirit. He restores my soul. He is the one who gently leads me back to that proper relationship with the Father. For that I am grateful. I do not ever want to have to face this world outside, out from under, the protection of the Holy Spirit. I've seen enough, done enough; know enough to realize that my dependency upon the Holy Spirit is my choice for living. Blessed be the name of the Lord!

Bible reference; Notes

1. Sing;

    <u>1 Chron. 16:23</u> –"Let the whole earth sing to the Lord. Each day proclaim the good news that He (Jesus) saves."

    <u>PS 47:7</u> –"For God is the King of all the earth. Sing praises with a skillful psalm."

    <u>Heb. 2:12</u> –"For He (Jesus) said to God, 'I will declare the wonder of your name to my brothers and sisters; I will praise (sing your praise) you among all your people.' "

2. Song;

    <u>PS 28:7</u> –"the Lord is my strength, my shield from every danger. I trust Him with all my heart. He helps me and my heart is filled with joy. I burst out in songs of thanksgiving."

    <u>Isa. 12:2</u> –"Behold, God is my salvation. I will trust and not be afraid, for the Lord God is my strength and song."

    <u>Isa. 42:10</u> –"Sing to the Lord a new song. Sing His praise from the ends of the earth."

3. Carnal;

    <u>Rom. 8:6</u> –"For the mind set on the flesh (carnal) is death, but the mind set on the Spirit is life and peace."

    <u>Rom. 8:7</u> –"For the sinful (carnal) nature is always hostile to God. It never did obey God's law and it never will."

    <u>2 Cor. 10:4</u> –"…for the weapons of our warfare are not of the flesh (carnal) but divinely powerful for the destruction (pulling down) of fortresses (strongholds)."

_____

_____

_____

_____

_____

_____

DAY 54

God, you have provided me with the ability to enter your presence at any moment. I am so grateful that you have afforded me such Grace and Mercy. In spite of everything, anything that goes on here during my day or night I have direct access to you through prayer. Sometimes I don't realize how easy it is for me to be in your presence, to contact you. I am always in your presence; you are on call 24/7. Where else can I get help like that? There is nothing here that can overtake me; there is nothing here that I can't handle. I am always in your presence, I feel protected, loved and cared for. When you meet all the needs in my life what is left for me to fear? Nothing, absolutely nothing.

It is so easy to stray from you and your Word. But, it is just as easy to remain in your light. I have to remember that the flesh, the natural me, the body is demanding one thing and my spirit man wants another. By listening to my Spirit man and allowing it to lead, I stay continually blessed. O Holy Spirit, help me to always follow your leading in my life.

Bible reference; Notes

1. Enter;
    > PS 100:4 –"Enter His gates with thanksgiving and His courts with praise. Give thanks to Him; bless His name for the Lord is good."
    >
    > Matt. 7:21 –"(Jesus' words) –"Not all people who sound religious are really godly. They may refer to me as Lord, but they still won't enter the Kingdom of Heaven."
    >
    > John 3:5 –"Jesus replied –'the truth is no one can enter the Kingdom of God without being born of water and the Spirit.' "

2. Presence;
    > PS 16:11 –"Thou will make known to me the path of life; in Thy presence is the fullness of joy."
    >
    > PS 23:5 –"You prepare a feast for me in the presence of my enemies. You welcome me as a guest."
    >
    > Luke 15:10 – (Jesus' words) –"In the same way, there I joy in the presence of God's angels when even one sinner repents."

3. Lead;
    > PS 5:8 –"Lead me in the right path O Lord, or my enemies will conquer me. Tell me clearly what to do and show me which way to turn."
    >
    > PS 25:5 –"Lead me by your truth and teach me, for you are the God who saves me. All day long I put my hope in you."
    >
    > Isa. 11:6 –"In that day, the wolf and lamb will live together; the leopard and the goat will be at peace. Calves and yearlings will be safe among lions, and a little child will lead them all."

_____

_____

_____

_____

_____

DAY 55

The Lord is most high over all the earth! He is my Rock; He hides me there in the cleft of the Rock and covers me there with His hand. That is a song. That song is in my heart. When I am in the Rock, I am safe, I am comfortable, and I feel secure. So much of my Christian upbringing has taught me not to trust feelings. But in the maturity of my Christian walk; I have learned to trust my feelings and to delight in them.

Intellect will get us so far. It builds the foundation for our knowledge of the Savior. The feelings we develop are from the confidence in our Savior. The feelings drive us to go deeper into our relationship, to seek out the Holy Spirit. I thank God for the emotional aspect of comfort, security, well-being, joy and peace of mind that we receive when we are close to the Lord. God created us as emotional beings. Those emotions can be used to confirm the blessings God has prepared for those who love Him. (Did you ever get a "lump in your throat" while listening to a touching story? There is nothing wrong with that.) Jesus, thank you for your work on earth. Thank you Holy Spirit for being in us and guiding and giving us comfort daily!

Bible reference; Notes

1. Rock;

    Deu. 32:4 –"He is the Rock. His work is perfect. Everything He does is just and fair, He is a faithful God who does no wrong, how just and upright He is."

    PS 18:2 –"the Lord is my rock, my fortress and my savior. My God is my rock in whom I find protection."

    1 Cor. 10:4 –"…and all of them drank the same miraculous water. For they all drank from the miraculous rock that traveled with them and that Rock was Christ."

2. Knowledge;

    1 Sam. 2:3 –"Boast no more so very proudly, do not let arrogance come out of your mouth; for the Lord is a God of knowledge and with Him actions are weighed."

    Prov. 1:7 –"Fear of the Lord is the beginning of knowledge. Only fools despise wisdom and discipline."

    Rom.11:33 –"Oh what a wonderful God we have! How great are His riches and wisdom and knowledge! How impossible it is for us to understand His decisions and His methods."

3. Savior;

    2 Sam. 22:3 –"My God, my rock in whom I take refuge. My shield and the horn of my salvation, my stronghold and my refuge; my savior, thou doth save me from violence."

    Isa. 43:3 –"For I am the Lord your God, the Holy One of Israel, your Savior…"

    2 Tim. 1:10 –"And now He has made all of this plain to us by the coming of Christ Jesus our Savior, who broke the power of death and showed us the way to everlasting life through the Good News."

_____

_____

_____

_____

_____

_____

DAY 56

Only the fool in his heart says there is no God. That I think comes out of Psalms. So, the connection is to April the first. There was a conversation about public holidays or days being set aside for recognition to celebrate historical events, minorities, presidents, seasons and so forth. The question was why there wasn't a day set aside for atheists? The judge studied the case evidence and carefully considered the lawyer's arguments. After doing so he sided against the plaintiff. His decision was that, indeed, there is already a day set aside for atheists; it is called April fool's Day.

God has blessed me this day because I am no fool. "Man does not live by bread alone, but every word that proceeds out of the mouth of God." In the beginning Christ came that I might have life and have it more abundantly. God spoke and it was so. God speaks to my very heart through the Holy Spirit. He calls me by name. He is the still small voice calling me. Holy Spirit, I hate to think what life would be like if I didn't have you to rely upon. If that were the case, I would be desperate above all men. It is better one day in your house than a thousand elsewhere.

Bible reference; Notes

1. Fool;

   <u>PS 14:1/53:1</u> –"Only fools say in their heart –'There is no God."

   <u>PS 92:5-6</u> –"O Lord what great miracles you do, and how deep are your thoughts. Only an ignorant person would not know this. Only a fool would not understand it.:"

   <u>Luke 12:20-21</u> –"But God said to him, 'You fool! You will die this very night. Then who will get it all? Yes, a person is a fool to store up earthly wealth but not have a rich relationship with God."

2. Heart;

   <u>Deu. 6:4-5</u> –"Hear O Israel! The Lord is our God, the Lord alone. You must love the Lord your God with all your heart, all your soul and all your strength."

   <u>1 Chron. 28:9</u> –"…worship and serve Him with your whole heart and with a willing mind. For the Lord sees every heart and understands and knows every plan and thought."

   <u>PS 51:10</u> –"Create in me a clean heart O God, renew a right spirit within me."

3. Bread;

   <u>Deu. 8:3</u> –"…He might make you understand that man does not live by bread alone…but everything that proceeds out of the mouth of the Lord."

   <u>John 6:35</u> –"Jesus replied, 'I am the Bread of Life, no one who comes to me will ever be hungry again…"

   <u>John 6:58</u> – Jesus speaking –"I am the true Bread from Heaven. Anyone who eats this bread will live forever…"

———————————————————————

———————————————————————

———————————————————————

———————————————————————

———————————————————————

DAY 57

Today was a good day. It was unstructured. I pretty much just goofed off. I stayed around the house and had the freedom to do what I wanted. There was no big brother looking over my shoulder.

There was no fear as I moved about in my daily business. I cooked outside, had no trouble getting meat from my refrigerator. I even went to town and bought groceries. I drove around to other small towns, paid for my groceries with a credit card. I bought what I wanted, where I wanted and when I wanted. God has truly blessed this nation! He has provided protection for me because of the connection (covenant) our Founding Fathers had with Him. This nation has been blessed for over two hundred years by God Himself.

We are one of the most free, prosperous and blessed nations in the world. Every day in His presence is a blessing. Every morning, just opening my eyes in this Nation, is a blessing. I want it to stay this way. But, I fear it will not. Already erosion has set into our established way of life. God has been assigned a back seat, or has even been removed, and replaced by the false wisdom of man. (Secular Humanism). It is even more than that. This Nation has become decidedly anti-Christian.

Bible reference; Notes

1. Free;

    <u>John 8:36</u> –"If therefore the Son (of God) shall make you free, you are free indeed."

    <u>Rom. 6:18</u> –"Now you are free from sin, your old master, and you have become slaves to your new master, righteousness."

    <u>Gal. 3:28</u> –"there is no longer Jew or Gentile, slave or free, male or female. For you are all Christians – you are one in Christ Jesus."

2. Fear;

    <u>PS 19:9</u> –"The fear of the Lord is clean, enduring forever. The judgments of the Lord are true, they are righteous altogether."

    <u>PS 23:23</u> –"You, who fear the Lord, praise Him."

    <u>Matt. 10:28</u> –"And do not fear those who kill the body, but are unable to kill the soul; but rather fear him who is able to destroy both soul and body in Hell."

3. Purchase;

    <u>Acts 8:20</u> –"But Peter replied, 'May your money perish with you for thinking God's gift can be bought (purchased)."

    <u>Acts 20:28</u> –"And now beware! Be sure you feed and shepherd God's flock – His church purchased with His blood…"

    <u>Eph. 1:14</u> –"The Spirit is God's guarantee that He will give us everything He promised and that He has purchased us to be His own people."

_____

_____

_____

_____

DAY 58

My joy this day comes in the form of my grandchildren. It is so good to see them growing and healthy. To see the strength in their bodies, the health in their minds and the normal functioning of their will is wonderful. It would be such a blessed thing if they could/would continue to maturity with such clear consciences and no strongholds to separate them from the Lord God Almighty.

Things in their lives right now are so uncomplicated. I pray that, as they gain knowledge of life, they would hear the "still small voice" of Christ and respond in a positive manner. When I think of the hazards and life traps that lay ahead for them, I take joy in the fact that they are loved by the Lord and have a future laid out for them.

What a comfort to be in the hands of a living God. Our God, Jehovah, has a path of life for them, a path of righteousness, waiting for each of them to follow. Their future is assured. All they need to do is to remain sensitive to His presence and obedient to His command. The Holy Spirit is here to guide them, protect them and care for them. What a great joy and assurance!

Bible reference; Notes

1. Generations;
    PS 33:11 – "The counsel of the Lord stands forever. He plans His heart from generation to generation."
    PS 100:5 – "For the Lord is good, His loving kindness is everlasting, and His faithfulness to all generations."
    1 Peter 2:9 – "but you are a chosen race (generation), a royal priesthood, a Holy Nation, a people for God's own possession…"

2. Children;
    PS 103:7 – "But the loving kindness of the Lord is from everlasting to everlasting in those who fear Him, and His righteousness to children's children." (Grandchildren)
    Matt. 18:3 – Jesus speaking – "Truly I say unto you, unless you are converted and become like children, you shall not enter into the Kingdom of Heaven."
    1 John 4:4 – "but you belong to God my dear children; you have already won your fight with these false prophets, because the Spirit that lives in you is greater than the spirit who lives in the world."

3. Separate;
    Matt. 25:32 – Jesus speaking – "And all the nations will be gathered before Him, and He will separate them from one another, as the shepherd separates the sheep from the goats and He will put the sheep on His right and the goats on His left…"
    Rom. 8:35 – "who shall separate us from the love of Christ…? I am convinced that neither death nor life nor angels…nor any created thing shall be able to separate us from the love of God, which is in Christ Jesus our Lord."

2 Cor. 6:17 – "Therefore come out from their midst and be separate, says the Lord."

_____

_____

_____

_____

_____

_____

DAY 59

The King is coming, the King is coming! Praise God He is coming for me! We celebrate Easter (Resurrection) Sunday because He was victorious over the grave. He is alive! He is our hope. This fulfills the hope of all generations. He is risen, and so shall we be!

In this He has given us a joy that is immeasurable. Our hope of eternal salvation rests in what He has done. I can think of no grater joy than to realize what He has in store for us - eternal life, and victory over the grave. The other part of this joy is to realize that the Holy Spirit abides with us on a daily basis. He, the Spirit, is with us here and now. The Son, the Father, abides in his home above. The Holy Spirit was given as the Comforter to live in us in the here and now. He is no farther away from us than a thought. He is the center of our being and constantly gives us assurance that all the Son said was true and is being carried out in us.

He is the earnest money, so to speak, that has been deposited in us, guaranteeing the return of the Son and His claim upon us when time on earth has been fulfilled. We have no greater joy than to realize God in His fullness will indeed keep all of His word. He is risen!

Bible reference; Notes

1. King;
> 1 Tim. 1:17 –"Glory and honor to God forever and ever, He is the eternal King, the unseen one who never dies; He alone is God. Amen."
>
> 1 Tim. 6:15 –"For at the right time Christ will be revealed from Heaven by the blessed and only almighty God, the King of kings and Lord of lords."
>
> Rev. 17:14 –"Together they will wage war against the Lamb, but the Lamb will defeat them because He is Lord over all lords and King over all kings…"

2. Alive;
> Rom. 6:4 –"For we died and were buried with Christ by baptism and just as Christ was raised from the dead (is alive) by the glorious power of the Father, now we also may have new lives."
>
> 1 Cor. 15:22 –"For as in Adam, all die, so also in Christ all shall be made alive."
>
> Rev. 1:17-18 – Jesus speaking –"…Do not be afraid, I am the First and the Last and the Living one. I was dead and behold I am alive forever more and I have the keys of death and Hades."

3. Grave;
> PS 30:3 –"You brought me up from the grave O Lord, you kept me from falling into the pit of death."
>
> PS 49:15 –"But as for me, God will redeem my life; He will snatch me up from the power of death." (The grave).
>
> 1 Cor. 15:51, 55 –"but let me tell you a wonderful secret…Not all…will die…all be transformed…at last…Death (the grave) is swallowed up in victory. O death, where is your victory? O death, where is your sting?"

_____

_____

_____

_____

_____

_____

DAY 60

Oh my God, you are good all the time. Holy Spirit, I thank you for your presence in my life. You are by my side night and day. Thank you for confirming your being in my life. I discovered, to me, a new truth about you in my personal life. When I was confronted with Your full presence and full truth, in that moment, I was in complete agreement, belief, tranquility, peace, of a sound mind, joyful, consciencous, willingness to obedience and confident of surrender to you in my life. I had a "hot flash", became completely relaxed and unconcerned about who or where I was. In that moment I was laid out on the floor gazing up and remembering your overwhelming presence in my being.

I now know that when one is in His presence and truth in such a personal way, it is perfectly fitting and proper to let go and celebrate this very personal encounter with the Holy Spirit. That was a new and very personal experience for me. Holy Spirit, I thank you very much. Contrived encounters like this may exist and abuse of it may be present. But my skepticism has gone away. We are human and we do exist in the realm of feelings and emotions. I think it is great that this happened to me. Lord, I praise your Holy name.

Bible reference; Notes

1. God;

> Matt. 4:10 – Jesus said –"For it is written 'you shall worship the Lord your God and serve Him only."
>
> Matt. 6:24 – Jesus speaking –"No one can serve two masters, for either he will hate the one and serve the other or he will hold to one and despise the other. You cannot serve God and mammon." (Man)
>
> Acts 15:12 –"And all the multitude kept silent and they were listening to Barnabas and Paul as they were relating what signs and wonders God had done through them among the Gentiles."

2. Spirit;

> John 4:24 –"God is spirit and those who worship Him must worship in Spirit and truth."
>
> John 6:63 –"It is the Spirit who gives life, the flesh profits nothing; the words that I have spoken to you are spirit and are life."
>
> Acts 2:4 –"And they were all filled with the Holy Spirit and began to speak with other tongues, as the Spirit was giving them utterance."

3. Truth;

> PS 25:5 –"Lead me by your truth and teach me, for you are the God who saves me. All day long I put my hope in you."
>
> John 3:21 –"But those who do what is right (practice the truth) come to the light gladly, so everyone can see that they are doing what God wants."
>
> 1 Tim. 6:3-5 –"…these (truths)… the sound wholesome teachings of the Lord Jesus Christ… are the foundation for a godly life…Anyone who teaches anything different…their minds are corrupt and they don't tell the truth."

Kenneth L. Canion

_____

_____

_____

_____

_____

_____

DAY 61

Every day, Lord, your Holy Spirit surrounds me. It is through spiritual eyes that I am aware of your presence in my life.

A walk through life without spiritual eyes would appear to be the same as a walk through life with no awareness of the eternal realm. One would go through the same movements, going to work, meeting obligations, eating and resting, as every other human being. However, what goes on the inside of one's soul would be completely different. One would have no assurance that all is not just meaningless repetition. However, I have a peace that passes all understanding. I have a goal, a place to go, a destination to follow and a purposeful life to live. I have a future that will last forever and I have a family waiting for me "on the other side."

I don't have to worry about stacking up wealth and possessions here on earth. It is all going to be changed, destroyed anyway. The presence of the Holy Spirit in my life has relieved me of such a burden that I have time to be joyful. I am thankful for what I do have. I am thankful for my life style. I'm just not pre-occupied with the things of this world, because I have a great eternal reward awaiting me!

Bible reference; Notes

1. Walk;

    PS 23:4 –"Even though I walk through the valley of the shadow of death I will fear no evil, for Thou are with me…"

    PS 56:13 –"For you have rescued me from death; you have kept my feet from slipping. So now I can walk in your presence O God, in your life giving light."

    John 8:12 –"Again therefore Jesus spoke to them saying – 'I am the light of the world; he who follows me shall not walk in the darkness, but shall have the light of life."

2. Eye;

    2 Chron. 16:9 –"For the eyes of the Lord move to and fro throughout the earth that He may strongly support those whose heart is completely His."

    PS 101:6 –"I will keep a protective eye upon the Godly so they may dwell with me in safety…"

    Eph. 1:18 –"I pray that the eyes of your heart may be enlightened so that you may know what is the hope of His calling , what are the riches of the glory of His inheritance in the saints."

3. Remain;

    John 9:41 –"If you were blind you would not be guilty,' Jesus replied, 'But you remain guilty because you claim you can see.'"

    1 Thes. 4:17 –"Then together with them, we who are still alive and remain on the earth will be caught up in the clouds to meet the Lord in the air and remain with Him forever."

    Heb. 4:9 –"There remains therefore a Sabbath rest (special rest) still waiting for the people of God."

DAY 62

I am experiencing a new love I have for the church family. In my new Spiritual eyes I have found out that there is a difference between just enjoying being around a group of people and loving them. Last night I realized that I love the people in our church. It is different than I had known before. I have begun to realize that we really are in the last days, "the age of the Gentiles" and it seems that these are the people with whom I will spend eternity.

It is like we are receiving our final assignments before the last quarter and have begun to recognize our individual responsibility to the team. "That's it; we've got to get it right. Run the play as written, I'll back you up." To me it is like those ballgames in high school when we would be breaking the huddle after the play had been called and we would glance at each other with an understanding look or give each other a thumbs up as we cinched our helmets, gripped our mouth piece and ran to assume the proper stance before the ball was snapped. It is a great feeling to know we are working together to usher in the return of our Great King, Jesus!

Bible reference; Notes

1. Love;

    <u>Deu. 6:4-5</u> –"Hear O Israel! The Lord is our God, the Lord alone. And you must love the Lord your God with all your heart, all your soul and all your strength."

    <u>Matt. 22:38-39</u> –"Jesus replied…'This is the first and greatest commandment. A second is equally important; Love your neighbor as yourself."

    <u>1 John 3:14</u> –"If we love our Christian brothers and sisters, it proves we have passed from death to eternal life. But a person who has no love is still dead."

2. Last;

    <u>Micah 4:1</u> –"In the last days the Temple of the Lord in Jerusalem will become the most important place on earth. People from all over the world will go there to worship."

    <u>John 6:40</u> –"For it is my father's will that all who see His Son and believe …should have eternal life – that I should raise them up in the last day." (From the dead)

    <u>2 Peter 3:3</u> –"First I want to remind you that in the last days there will be scoffers who will laugh at the truth and do every evil thing they desire."

3. Eternal;

    <u>John 3:14-15</u> – Jesus speaking –"As Moses lifted up the bronze snake on a pole in the wilderness so I, the Son of Man, must be lifted up on a pole so that everyone who believes in me will have eternal life."

    <u>John 5:39</u> – Jesus speaking –"You search the scriptures because you believe they give you eternal life. But the Scriptures point to me."

    <u>Rev. 22:12</u> – Jesus speaking –"See, I am coming soon and my reward is with me, to repay all according to their deeds."

Kenneth L. Canion

_____

_____

_____

_____

_____

_____

DAY 63

It is your consistency, God. I am blessed so much by your consistency. "Day unto day utters speech; night unto night shows forth knowledge." In order to hide from you, or the evidence of your presence, one has to be completely dead in the Spirit. Just looking around, noticing the day, gives enough evidence for belief. Before I get too prideful, I know you knew me as I was knitted together in my mother's womb. Before time began you called my name, you knew in what era I would live, in what country I would be born and you even knew who would be my parents.

You, God, placed that belief in me! Thank you. Praise your Holy Name. What would I have done with eternity without you? I shudder at the thought of facing life alone and without the Holy Spirit to guide and guard me. I count my blessings daily, Lord. I know, in the natural, I could not have obtained the level of my earthly achievement. I would have been distracted or ambushed by some worldly lust and remained a prisoner to a stronghold of some kind. (There are thousands of traps out there, just pick one.) When I realize how helpless man truly is against the Prince of the Power of the Air, without Christ, I tremble. Thank God I've been changed, set free!

Bible reference; Notes

1. Change;

    <u>1 Cor.15:51-53</u> –"But let me tell you a secret…Not all of us will die, but we will all be (changed)…And then we who are living will be changed so that we will never die."

    <u>2 Cor. 3:16-18</u> –"But whenever anyone turns to the Lord…He gives freedom…and as the Spirit of the Lord works within us we become more and more like Him (changed into His likeness) and reflect His glory even more."

    <u>Phil. 3:21</u> –"He will take these weak mortal bodies of ours and change them into glorious bodies like His own, using the same mighty power that He will use to conquer everything everywhere."

2. Knowledge;

    <u>Matt. 6:8</u> –"…your Father knows (has knowledge of) exactly what you need even before you ask Him!"

    <u>Rom. 8:17</u> –"And the Father who knows all hearts knows what the Spirit is saying, for the Spirit pleads for us believers in harmony with God's own will."

    <u>2 Tim. 2:19</u> –"But God's truth stands firm…The Lord knows those who are His…Those who claim they belong to the Lord must turn away from all wickedness."

3. Freedom;

    <u>Rom. 6:7</u> –"For when we died with Christ we were set free from the power of sin."

    <u>1 Cor. 2:12</u> –"Now we have received not the spirit of the world, but the Spirit who is from God that we might know the things freely given to us by God."

<u>Rev. 22:17</u> –"And the Spirit and the bride say come. And let the one who hears say come. And let the one who is thirsty come, let the one who wishes to take the water of life without cost." (Freely)

_____

_____

_____

_____

_____

_____

DAY 64

As each day passes I realize how faithful God is to us. In my total life, from birth until now, God has continually blessed me with provision and protection. I am completely overwhelmed by the amount of love He has poured out just for me, only one of His believers. If I could praise Him and worship continuously from now until the end of my life, it would not even begin to be adequate for what He has done for me, for all of mankind.

When I look past the matters of life here and consider time in eternity I can understand how God's Word tells us we are but a puff of smoke, a vapor in the morning. It is really too much to consider. How and why did God bless me like He has done? What did I ever do to deserve even one of His blessings? When I consider the heavens, the sun, moon, the stars that He has made, it makes me wonder what is man, who am I that you, O Lord consider me! Happiness is within me because I realize that all else will fail. Life, as we know it, will end, change will come. But His word will remain forever. Jesus, our Rock, is unmovable. He is our cornerstone.

Bible reference; Notes

1. Eternal;

   Deu. 33:27 –"The eternal God is your refuge and His everlasting arms are under you. He thrusts out the enemy before you."

   Mark 10:29-30 –"Jesus replied – 'I assure you that everyone who has given up house… brothers…sisters…children or property for my sake…will receive…a hundred times over…and eternal life."

   John 17:3 –"Jesus speaking –"And this is the way to have eternal life – to know You, the only true God and Jesus Christ, the one You sent to earth."

2. Morning;

   PS 5:3 –"Listen to my voice in the morning Lord. Each morning I bring my requests to you and wait expectantly."

   PS 59:16 –"Bur as for me, I will sing about your power, I will shout with joy each morning because of your unfailing love."

   Lam. 3:23 –"Great is His faithfulness. His mercies begin afresh each day." (Morning)

3. Rock;

   Deu. 32:3-4 –"I will proclaim the name of the Lord…He is the Rock, His work is perfect. Everything He does is just and fair. He is a faithful God."

   PS 40:1-2 –"I waited patiently for the Lord to help me…He lifted me out of the pit of despair, out of the mud and mire. He set my feet on solid ground." (A rock)

Rom. 9:32-33 –"…They stumbled over the great rock in their path. God warned them when He said, 'I am placing a stone in Jerusalem that causes people to stumble and a rock that makes them fall…anyone who believes in Him will not be disappointed."

_____

_____

_____

_____

_____

_____

DAY 65

God is good all the time. He blesses us in ways of which we are not even aware. His eye is consistently upon us. He is continually searching the earth to find those whose heart is right toward Him. What we do, what we believe, does not escape Him. He rewards those whose heart is right toward Him.

I feel that I am blessed in all areas of my life. He has rewarded me in body and spirit. Yesterday while my wife was at a "jewelry party," I decided to see if I could still run (jog) as I used to before I broke my foot and got lazy. It was during the long recuperation that I got out of the practice of jogging or any physical exercise, because the pain was so persistent. Well, praise God, I could still do it! My body remained strong enough during those "off" years and I am still able to jog. I used to say that by jogging on a regular basis, I was investing in life insurance. Thank the Lord, I was right. Keeping my physical body in shape brings its rewards. Keeping my spiritual body in shape brings rewards also. Since spending more time with the Holy Spirit, I find my strength here has increased. Just trust God. He does what He says!

Bible reference; Notes

1. Everlasting;

    Gen. 9:16 –"When I see the rainbow in the clouds, I will remember the eternal (everlasting) covenant between God and every living creature on earth."

    PS 145:13 –"For Your kingdom is an everlasting kingdom. You rule generation after generation."

    Isa. 26:4 –"Trust in the Lord always, for the Lord God is the eternal (everlasting) Rock." (Strength)

2. Search;

    PS 139:23 –"Search me O God and know my heart, test me and know my thoughts."

    Jer. 29:13 –"If you look (search) for me in earnest, you will find me when you seek me."

    Lam. 3:40 –"…let us examine (search) our ways. Let us turn again in repentance to the Lord."

3. Reward;

    Matt. 5:12 – Jesus' words –"Be happy…be very glad! For a great reward awaits you in heaven…"

    Matt. 6:6 – Jesus' words –"But when you pray, go away by yourself, shut the door behind you, and pray to your Father secretly. Then your Father who knows all secrets will reward you."

    Heb. 10:35 –"Do not throw away this confident trust in the Lord no matter what happens. Remember the great reward it brings you."

DAY 66

God rebuilds lives, relationships and keeps us safe. I love Psalms 91. "He who dwells in the shelter of the most high will rest in the shadow of the Almighty."

Tonight at the college we were privileged to see two lives reunited. They had been going through an awful time. The spirit of darkness had been plaguing their marriage and their family. She had separated herself from her husband and from our class. Satan had pretty much wrecked their lives. Praise God, His love, mercy, grace and holiness overcame all else and restored their lives! What we saw was a restoration, an answer to prayer right before our very eyes. Thank you, Jesus, for your powerful and mighty work. Oh, Lord, you take interest in the least of us. Your promises are true for all of us. Your focus is upon each individual, one person at a time.

The magnitude, the glory of your love is unfathomable. Your ways are far beyond man's ways. Oh, God, you are so holy. I will never be able to understand or see the complete greatness of your love for us. It is just too much to understand. Thank you Lord, thank you Jesus, thank you Holy Spirit, for your working in every single life, for your faithfulness to our prayers, for your sacrifice!

Bible reference; Notes

1. Return/restore;

    <u>Jer. 30:17</u> –"For I will restore you to health and I will heal you of your wounds, declares the Lord."

    <u>PS 23:1&3</u> –"The Lord is my shepherd…He restores my soul."

    <u>Mal. 3:7</u> –"Ever since the days of your ancestors you have scorned my laws and failed to obey them. Now return unto me and I will return to you, says the Lord Almighty."

2. Safe;

    <u>PS 119:116-117</u> –"Lord, sustain me as you promised that I may live. Do not let my hopes be crushed. Sustain me and I will be saved." (Safe)

    <u>Prov. 18:10</u> –"The name of the Lord is a strong fortress, the godly run to Him and are safe."

    <u>Prov. 3:21 & 23 –</u>"My child, don't lose sight of good planning and insight…they keep you safe on your way and keep your feet from stumbling."

3. Cleave;

    <u>Gen. 2:23-24</u> –"At last, Adam exclaimed. She is part of my own flesh and bone…This explains why a man leaves his father and mother and is joined to (cleaves to) his wife."

    <u>Josh. 22:5</u> –"…Love the Lord your God, walk in all His ways, obey His commands, be faithful to Him (cleave to Him) and serve Him with all your heart and all your soul."

    <u>Rom. 12:9</u> –"Don't just pretend that you love others, really love them. Hate what is wrong. Stand on the side (cleave that which is) of good."

Kenneth L. Canion

_____

_____

_____

_____

_____

DAY 67

The things I notice today that are a blessing to me from you, Lord, are wonderful. I see a picture of myself in my truck, just about to leave for work. The day is bright; I see vivid colors, blue sky with pure white, wispy clouds. The green contrast of the grass and trees stand out as a beauty to behold. I smell the wonderful odor of the cut pecan wood as it sits in the wood rack. Most of all I see my mate, my wife, standing there with a beautiful smile, as I pull out. Her warm eyes and accepting, approving, reassuring countenance bid me a good trip and successful day.

God, you have blessed me so much. I often am overwhelmed at your care and concern for a single individual. How great you are, how wonderful are your precepts, and how perfect are your laws. The more I depend on you, the more you provide. The more I trust you, the more you prove yourself. How or why you do such, I cannot fathom. I pray that everyone would receive the same blessings I have in this life. God, you are so great! My words can only repeat themselves. I am powerless to express the love you have poured into me.

Kenneth L. Canion

Bible reference; Notes

1. Wonderful;
   PS 40:5 –"O Lord my God, you have done many miracles for us. Your plans for us are too numerous to list. If I tried to recite all your wonderful deeds I would never come to the end of them."
   PS 114:4 –"Who can forget the wonders He performs? How gracious and merciful is our Lord."
   Isa. 25:1 –"O Lord I will honor and praise your name, for you are my God. You do such wonderful things."

2. Vision;
   Prov. 29:18 –"Where there is no vision, the people are unrestrained (perish). But happy is he who keeps the law." (My ways)
   Joel 2:28 –"…I will pour out my Spirit on all people. Your sons and daughters will prophecy, your old men will dream dreams, and your young men will see visions."
   Acts 2:17 –"In the last days, God said –'I will pour out my Spirit upon all people. Your sons and daughters will prophesy, your young men will see visions and your old men will dream dreams."

3. Lord;
   Deu. 10:12 –"…what does the Lord your God require of you? He requires you to fear Him, to live according to His will, to love and worship Him with all your heart and soul."
   Judges 6:10 –"I told you, 'I am the Lord your God.' "
   PS 13:6 – I will sing to the Lord, because He has been so good to me."

200

_____

_____

_____

_____

_____

DAY 68

"The Lord livith and blessed be the Rock, blessed be the Rock of my salvation." That is my song for the day, it brings me great pleasure. I am in the world and know that the forces of man's dominion are overwhelming to me and my loved ones. It is only by the Grace of God that we succeed here and can pursue our individual lives in relative freedom from oppression by the government or any other agency.

When I consider the way things are in most of the world, things like controlling cartels, despots, dictators or military juntas I am extremely grateful to God Almighty. We viewed some video of the Holocaust in school. In it I saw man's inhumanity to man, the anxious faces, the lost lives, the extreme sorrow and pain. If all mankind would just turn their faith and trust to the Lord, there would not be a possibility of horrors like that happening again. But, I think it will happen. In fact, I see in God's word the condition of the world during the Great Tribulation. Even that gives me reason to praise God and be joyful in Him. He has created us for Himself. Those who call upon the Lord shall be saved! Thank God we will be called out before this happens.

Bible reference; Notes

1. Lives;

    2 Sam. 22:47 –"The Lord lives! Blessed be my Rock, may the God of my salvation be exalted!

    Job 19:25 –"But as for me, I know that my Redeemer lives, and that He will stand upon the earth at last."

    John 11: 25-26 –"Jesus said…I am the resurrection and the life; he who believes in me shall live, even if he dies and everyone who lives and believes in Me shall never die…"

2. Dominion;

    Dan. 7:27 –"Then the sovereignty, power (dominion) and greatness of all the kingdoms under heaven will be given to the holy people of the Most High. They will rule (have dominion) forever…"

    Rom. 6:9 –"We are sure of this because Christ rose from the dead and He will never die again. Death no longer has any power (dominion) over Him."

    Eph. 1:21 –"Now He is far above any ruler or authority or power (dominion) or leader or anything else in this world or in the world to come."

3. Grace;

    1 Cor. 1:3 –"May God our Father and the Lord Jesus Christ give you His grace and peace."

    Col. 3:16 –"Let the word of Christ dwell richly within you, with all wisdom, teaching and admonishing one another with psalms and hymns and spiritual songs, singing with thankfulness (grace) in your hearts to God.:

    Heb. 4:16 –"Let us therefore draw near with confidence to the throne of grace that we may receive mercy and find grace to help in times of need."

Kenneth L. Canion

_____

_____

_____

_____

_____

_____

DAY 69

We all thank and praise God for good things that happen to us on a daily basis. What about those things that we can't see, what about those things that didn't happen to us? We are covered by the blood of Jesus. We are walking in His light daily. If we could see in the spirit realm, would we witness great battles that occur on our behalf that protect us from these unseen forces?

This kind of thinking was made clear to me in a book I read about spiritual reality. I don't really want to see what "might have been" if it were not for the love and protection of the Lord, God Almighty. I believe I would be too frightened to move. But, I am aware, because of His Word, that we battle not against flesh and blood, but against powers and principalities. Praise God, Jesus has got my back!

It is hard enough just to walk in the physical realm. Seeing the other dimension operation around me would be more than I could bear. I am completely humbled when I realize the cost and attention God has poured into me, an insignificant spot on a mosaic of immense proportions! From Adam to all the human beings ever born, how could He know me? Praise God, He gave it all for me!

Bible reference; Notes

1. Sight;

   <u>Deu. 12:28</u> –"Be careful to listen to all these words…in order that it may be will with you …for you will be doing what is good and right in the sight of the Lord your God."

   <u>1 Kings 11:38</u> –"then it will be that, if you listen, …and walk in My ways and do what is right in My sight…I will be with you…"

   <u>James 4:10</u> –"Humble yourself in the presence (sight) of the Lord and He will exalt you."

2. Battle;

   <u>PS 18:39</u> –"You have armed me with strength for the battle; You have subdued my enemies under my feet."

   <u>PS 55:18</u> –"He will redeem my soul in peace from the battle which is against me."

   <u>2 Chron. 32:7-8</u> –"Be strong and courageous! Don't be afraid…they are just men. We have the Lord our God to help us and to fight our battles for us!"

3. Flesh;

   <u>PS 56:3-4</u> –"When I am afraid I will put my trust in You. O God, I praise your Word, I trust in God; so why should I be afraid? What can mere mortals (flesh) do to me?"

   <u>Matt. 26:41</u> – Jesus' words - "Keep alert and pray, otherwise temptation will over power you. For though the spirit is willing enough, the body (flesh) is weak."

   <u>John 6:63</u> – Jesus' words – "It is the Spirit who gives eternal life. Human effort (the flesh) accomplishes nothing."

_____

_____

_____

_____

_____

_____

Day 70

Today is Income Tax day! What could be good about that? God has blessed us individually in this nation. My wife and I have been blessed all our life. We have always made enough money to be able to pay income taxes. If you look at it in a certain way it can be considered a blessing. Lord God I thank you for allowing us to thus far be sheltered in a country that provides protection for its citizens. I thank you for the process our forefathers went through in order to form the "One Nation Under God." I believe it is that covenant relationship with You by our founders that enabled us to last this long as a representative democracy, concerned with the welfare of its citizens.

I shudder to think what path we, as a nation, are taking now. I am no longer sure that our national leaders have our best interest in mind. It appears to me that this administration is bound and determined to do away with that godly covenant and relationship with our Creator. It seems that we, as a nation, are dashing headlong to a secular humanism existence with freedoms only as the state allows and not those "inalienable rights" in our Constitution. All worries set aside, God is still in control!

Bible reference; Notes

1. Bless;

   <u>1 Chron. 3:9-10</u> –"There was a man named Jabez…
   who prayed to the God of Israel…Oh that you
   would bless me and extend my land…and God
   granted him his request."

   <u>PS 5:11-12</u> –"But let all who take refuge in you
   rejoice…Protect them…For You bless the godly O
   Lord, surrounding them with your shield of love."

   <u>PS 103:1</u> –"Bless the Lord, Oh my soul; and all that
   is within me bless His holy name."

2. Protect;

   <u>Deu. 32:37-39</u> –"Where now are their (other) gods…
   let them rise up and help (protect) you. See now that
   I am He and there is no other God besides me."

   <u>PS 61:2-4</u> –"Lead me to the towering rock of safety,
   for you are my safe refuge…a fortress…safe beneath
   the shelter of your wings."

   <u>PS 62:5-6</u> –"I wait quietly before God, for my hope
   is in Him. He alone is my rock and my salvation,
   my fortress where I will not be shaken."

3. Creator;

   <u>Isa. 40:28</u> –"Have you never heard or understood?
   Don't you know that the Lord is the everlasting
   God, the Creator of all the earth?

   <u>Rom. 1:20</u> –"From the time the world was created
   people have seen…all that God has made. They can
   clearly see His invisible qualities – His eternal power
   and divine nature…they have no excuse…"

   <u>Rom. 1:25</u> –"Instead of believing what they knew
   was the truth about God; they…chose to believe a
   lie…worshipped the things God made, but not the
   Creator Himself."

Kenneth L. Canion

_____

_____

_____

_____

_____

_____

DAY 71

Thank you Lord, I sense security and safety in Your presence. I know from Your Word that when all else fails and every other opportunity proves false, You are steady; You are my rock. I know my physical life is in Your hands and I know I have choices I can make concerning my health and welfare. The most important choice is to place my spiritual life in you where it is everlasting and completely safe and secure. Your presence in me comforts me. I am established for eternity and am very thankful for that.

I pray that I may be able to pass on that same security to my children and their families. Lord, I thank you for my grandchildren. They are precious to me and I know they are a joy in your sight. I believe it is by Your love and concern that they have developed healthy and whole thus far. I take comfort that you have planned a future for each one. I am blessed in knowing that every aspect of their lives has been planned and is waiting for them in time to fulfill as your perfect will. Thank you for your promised Word. In the name of Jesus I bind their minds to the mind of Christ and bind their will to the will of God.

Bible reference; Notes

1. Present;

    PS 46:1 –"God is our refuge and strength, a very present help in trouble."

    Rom. 8:38 –"For I am convinced that neither death, nor life, nor angels, nor principalities, nor powers, nor things present, nor things to come, shall be able to separate us from the love of God, which is in Christ Jesus our Lord."

    Gal. 1:4 –"He died for our sins, just as God our Father planned, in order to rescue us from this (present) evil world…"

2. Word;

    Jer. 1:12 –"Then the Lord said to me, 'You have seen well, for I am watching over My Word to perform it.'"

    Matt. 4:4 – Jesus' words- "It is written, man shall not live on bread alone, but on every word that proceeds out of the mouth of God."

    Matt. 12:36 – Jesus' words –"And I say unto you that every careless word that men shall speak, they shall render account for it in the Day of Judgment."

3. Steadfast;

    1 Cor. 15:58 –"So, my dear brothers and sisters, be strong and steady (steadfast) always enthusiastic about the Lord's work, for you know that nothing you do for the Lord is ever useless."

    Heb. 3:14 –"For if we are faithful (steadfast) to the end, trusting God just as firmly as when we first believed, we will share in all that belongs to Christ."

    1 Peter 5:9 –"Take a firm stand against him (Satan) and be strong in your faith (steadfast). Remember that your Christian brothers and sisters… are going through the same kind of suffering you are."

_____

_____

_____

_____

_____

_____

DAY 72

Today, for me, is a day of celebration. It is the date of my birth, physical birth. It was a pleasant day. Yesterday we were blessed with a wonderful visit to my son and grandchildren. In them I can see God's many blessings. This fulfills the promise of God in Psalms 112, verses one and two where it says that the children of those who fear (love) the Lord will be successful. We were blessed with healthy, whole grandchildren because of the promise of God.

This day we spent with our church family, with a great meal together at a restaurant. There is so much coverage and blessing in being a member of the Body of Christ. Lunch was followed by a nap at home in the afternoon and then on to our church college class. When we are gathered in God's name and study His Word, blessings abound. It has reached the level of "awesome." Hearing God's Word, reading and studying it, sharing it and seeing the evidence of its effect in other people's lives is an almost unbelievable experience. Just being a part of the growth in other's lives as they undergo change related to The Word is just wonderful. We share our lives, feelings, tears and love. It is, in that class, as it should be in churches all across this land. All pretenses have been removed. We see and feel the workings of the Holy Spirit in each other's lives! It is great and I could not have had a better birthday celebration.

Bible reference; Notes

1. Fear;
   > PS 2:11 –"Serve the Lord with reverent fear and rejoice with trembling."
   >
   > PS 25:14 –"Friendship with the Lord is reserved for those who fear Him. With them He shares the secrets of His covenant."
   >
   > 2 Cor. 7:1 –"Because we have these promises…let us cleanse ourselves from everything that can defile our body or spirit. And let us work toward complete purity because we fear the Lord."

2. Love;
   > John 13:34 –"So now I am giving you a new commandment. Love each other, just as I have loved you, you should love each other."
   >
   > Rom 5:8 –"But God showed His great love toward us by sending Christ to die for us while we were yet sinners."
   >
   > 1 John 4:18 –"Such love has no fear because perfect love expels all fear."

3. Strength;
   > PS 28:7 –"the Lord is my strength, my shield from every danger, I trust in Him with all my heart."
   >
   > PS 29:11 –"The Lord gives His people strength. The Lord blesses them with peace."
   >
   > PS 105:4 –"Search for the Lord and all His strength and keep on searching."

_____

_____

_____

DAY 73

Your Word, God, is a light unto my feet and a lamp unto my path. It is daytime and I can see in the physical realm, but Your Word is required for me to be able to really see and stay on your path. In the flesh I fail, I fall and falter. It is a never ending battle for me to stay "tuned in" to the Holy Spirit. I have a tendency to wander, to follow after the natural desires of my flesh. No matter how much I will to remain righteous, I fail. God, you offer me a constant "pick-me-up."

I understand now how man was condemned by the law. We cannot remain righteous, no matter how hard we try. Thank you, God that you have provided for us. It is through your righteousness alone that we are saved daily from our own failures. You alone save us. If there ever comes a day when we can't think of something good that you have done for us, we have gone completely blind to Your Word. That is called walking in darkness and that darkness is very deep. Praise God that Christ has provided it all for us. He was crucified for all of us, me included. The light of His Word penetrated that darkness. I receive it Lord Jesus!

Bible reference; Notes

1. Path;

   <u>PS 16:11</u> –"You (Lord) will show me the way (path) of life, granting me the joy of your presence and the pleasures of living with you forever."

   <u>PS 119:105</u> –"Your word is a lamp for my feet and a light for my path."

   <u>Prov. 4:14</u> –"Do not do as the wicked do or follow the path of evildoers."

2. Flesh;

   <u>Mark 14:38</u> – Jesus' words –"Keep alert and pray. Otherwise temptation will overpower you. For though the spirit is willing enough, the body (flesh) is weak."

   <u>Rom. 8:13</u> –"For if you keep on following it (the flesh) you will perish. But if, through the power of the Holy Spirit, you turn from it (the flesh) and its evil deeds, you will live."

   <u>Gal. 2:20</u> –"I have been crucified with Christ and it is no longer I who live, but Christ lives in me, and the life which I now live in the flesh, I live by faith in the Son of God, who loved me and delivered Himself up for me."

3. Desire;

   <u>PS 145:6</u> –"When you (Lord) open your hand you satisfy the hunger and thirst of every living thing."

   <u>Mark 11:24</u> – Jesus' words –"Listen to me! You can pray for anything (your desire) and if you believe, you will have it."

   <u>Col. 1:9</u> –"So we have continued praying for you ever since we first heard about you. We ask God to give you a complete understanding of what He wants to do in your lives and we ask Him to make you wise (desire) in spiritual wisdom."

_____

_____

_____

_____

_____

_____

DAY 74

God sustains me. His repetitive mercy and care for me are inexhaustible. He never runs out of blessings for me. Day follows day, night unto night, and year after year. I mature, grow old as time passes and yet the daily blessings are as fresh as they were the first day I received! It is amazing! From my finite view point I cannot even imagine the consistency of my God. He is awesome, Holy, Almighty and ever present. I do not have to worry about Him leaving me. I can count on the presence of His blessings, His protection, the Holy Spirit and the freshness of my salvation every day, every second, every moment.

I know for certain that if I get out from under the protection of His Wings it is not He who has withdrawn, it is me. There is no aspect of my life He has not already covered for me. There is no problem that can occur that He has not already perfected a solution. There is no circumstance where He has not already created an alternative for me. He has my back! When a person is covered that well, all that person can do is praise the Lord. Father I thank you for the joy You have put in my life because of your love for me. Hallelujah!

Bible reference; Notes

1. Mercy;

    <u>PS 106:1</u> –"Praise the Lord! O give thanks to the Lord, for He is good. For His loving kindness (mercy) is everlasting."

    <u>Eph. 2:4</u> –"But God is so rich in mercy and He loved us so very much that even while we were dead because of our sins, He gave us life when He raised Christ from the dead."

    <u>1 Peter 2:10</u> –"Once you were not a people, but now you are the people of God; you had not received mercy, but now you have received mercy."

2. Everlasting;

    <u>Isa. 60:19</u> –"No longer will you need the sun or moon to give you light, for the Lord your God will be your everlasting light and He will be your glory."

    <u>Jer. 10:10</u> –"But the Lord is the only true God, the living God. He is the everlasting King!"

    <u>John 5:24</u> – Jesus' words – "I assure you, those who listen to my message and believe in God who sent me, have eternal (everlasting) life. They will never be condemned for their sins, but they have already passed from death to life."

3. Holy Spirit;

    <u>Matt. 3:11</u> –"I baptize with water those who turn from their sin and turn to God. But someone is coming…He will baptize you with the Holy Spirit and with fire."

    <u>Luke 3:22</u> – Speaking of Jesus –"…and the Holy Spirit descended on Him in the form of a dove. And a voice from Heaven said 'You are my beloved Son, and I am fully pleased with you."

<u>Luke 11:13</u> – Jesus' words –"If you sinful people know how to give good gifts to your children, how much more will your Heavenly Father give the Holy Spirit to those who ask Him?"

_____

_____

_____

_____

_____

_____

DAY 75

Father, I realize you are in every aspect of life in everyone in existence. There is not one of your creations that you do not love. There is not one person for whom you did not lay down your life. I thank you for that, because that includes me and it includes all of our children and their offspring. That is everybody. Your love is available for all! Thank you.

In my work I see the condition of students in my classroom. I see the strongholds that have been erected in their lives. I see the manifest behavior that results when they try to compensate for a life without the love of Christ present in them. Quite truthfully, they are a mess. I pity them, I long for their salvation and I pray for them. But, they continue to live day to day with the power of the great liar in their lives. The love of Christ is not in place in their lives. They manifest bizarre behavior and become their own worst enemy. I don't know why they are trapped in such a life. I do know the answer for them. They have the freedom to choose, but it seems that they would rather believe a lie than the truth. God please have mercy and grant them a revelation of You. Thank you Father, you have provided us with salvation through Jesus Christ, not based on our righteousness, but yours!

Bible reference; Notes

1. Sacrifice;

> <u>Mark 10:45</u> – Jesus speaking –"For even I, the Son of Man, came here not to be served but to serve others and to give my life as a ransom (sacrifice) for many."
>
> <u>1 Tim. 2:5-6</u> –"For there is only one God and one Mediator who can reconcile God and people. He is the man Christ Jesus. He gave (sacrificed) His life to purchase freedom for everyone."
>
> <u>Heb. 9:26</u> –"…But no, He came once for all time, at the end of the age, to remove the power of sin forever by His sacrificial death for us."

2. Love;

> <u>Deu. 7:9</u> –"Understand therefore that the Lord your God is indeed God. He is the faithful God who keeps His covenant for a thousand generations and…loves those who love Him and obey His commandments."
>
> <u>Eph. 2:4-5</u> –"But God is so rich in mercy and He loved us so very much that even while we were dead because of our sins, He gave us life when He raised Christ from the dead."
>
> <u>1 John 4:9-10</u> –"God showed us how much He loved us by sending His only Son…This is real love. It is not that we loved God, but that He loved us and sent His son as a sacrifice to take away our sins."

3. Deceive;

> <u>Matt. 24:4-5</u> – Jesus speaking –"Don't let anyone mislead (deceive) you. For many will come in my name saying 'I am the Messiah.' They will lead many astray."

Gal. 6:7 –"Don't be misled (deceived). Remember you can't ignore God and get away with it. You will always reap what you sow."

Rev. 20:10 –"Then the Devil, who betrayed (deceived) them was thrown into the Lake of Fire that burns with sulfur…There they will be tormented…forever and ever."

_____

_____

_____

_____

_____

_____

DAY 76

Your promise O Lord lasts forever. In that I am glad. In that I am secure. These are troubling times for the U.S.A. in terms of politics, public trust in our system and confidence in the continuation of this "One Nation under God". The president and his regime are "hell-bent" to transform this nation from one with a covenant relationship with God, the Creator, to one of human engineered justice and redistribution of wealth. There have been many breaches of the "contract" with our Lord over the decades and now this administration is by-passing the Constitution with executive orders, more than all the other presidents put together. In addition there has been the appointment, by executive order, of over thirty-nine czars who answer to nothing and no one except the president.

My point of confusion is whether this is all in God's timing and Bible prophecy or whether it is just an egomaniac getting his way with crooked "behind closed door" deals and outright deception of the American public. He has created so many crises and extreme changes that it baffles the average citizen who, I am afraid, is being duped. Our nation has fallen so far away from that covenant relationship with God that we have brought this upon ourselves. But, nothing compares to the promises we have in Him!

Bible reference; Notes

1. Promise;
    > <u>Acts 2:38-39</u> –"…Each of you must turn from your sins and turn to God, and be baptized in the name of Jesus Christ…then…receive the Holy Spirit. This promise is to you…all who have been called…"
    >
    > <u>Acts 13:23</u> –"And it is one of King David's descendants, Jesus, who is God's promised Savior…"
    >
    > <u>Rom. 4:14</u> –"So if you claim that God's promise is (only) for those who obey God's law and think they are 'good enough' in God's sight then you are saying that faith is useless."

2. Glad;
    > <u>PS 67:4</u> –"How glad the nations will be, singing for joy, because you (Lord) govern them with justice and direct the actions of the whole world."
    >
    > <u>Matt. 5:12</u> –"Be happy about it! Be very glad! For a great reward awaits you in heaven. And remember the ancient prophets were persecuted too!
    >
    > <u>1 Peter 4:13</u> –"Instead be very glad – because these trials will make you partners with Christ in His suffering and afterward…joy of sharing His glory… displayed to the whole world."

3. Nation;
    > <u>Deu. 4:7</u> –"For what great nation has God as near to them as the Lord our God is near to us whenever we call on Him?"
    >
    > <u>PS 33:12</u> –"What joy for the nation whose God is the Lord, whose people He has chosen for His own."
    >
    > <u>Matt. 24:7</u> – Jesus' words –"The nations and kingdoms will proclaim war against each other, and there will be famines and earthquakes in many parts of the world."

_____

_____

_____

_____

_____

_____

DAY 77

The Lord liveth and blessed be the Rock, blessed be the God of my salvation. No matter what happens here, that statement is always true. There is nothing that can overcome God. He was, is and evermore shall be the savior of my soul. His word endures forever, regardless of circumstances. I can be overcome, over-whelmed and buried completely by the "stuff" that goes on from day to day and yet I am safe in Him. O God, I am so grateful, so thankful that You have it all figured out. Not only that, but You have also computed me in the outcome and have provided victory for me and all those who love you and seek your face.

There is so much comfort in you Lord. I can never figure out why you chose to reveal yourself to me, but I am eternally grateful to you! Thank you for being wounded for my transgressions and bruised for my iniquities. By your stripes I have been healed. Until recently I just glanced pass those words. Now I have more appreciation for their meaning. There is not a day, not a moment in time when I am not being continually blessed by your presence. Thank you, Father, for your presence.

Bible reference; Notes

1. Overcome;

   John 16:33 – Jesus speaking –"I have told you all this so that you may have peace in me. Here on earth you will have many trials and sorrows. But take heart because I have overcome the world."

   Rom. 12:21 –"Do not be overcome by evil (the world), but overcome evil with good."

   1 John 4:4 –"You are from God…and have overcome them (the world); because greater is He that is in you than he who is in the world."

2. Victory;

   PS 98:1 –"Sing a new song to the Lord, for He has done wonderful deeds. He has won a mighty victory by His power and holiness."

   Isa. 25:8 –"He (the Lord) will swallow up death for all times (in victory) and the Lord God will wipe tears away from all faces…He will remove the reproach of His people from all the earth."

   1 John 5:4 –"For every child of God defeats this evil world by trusting Christ to give the victory."

3. Seek;

   1 Chron. 16:10-11 –"Glory in His holy name. Let the heart of those who seek the Lord be glad. Seek the Lord and His strength. Seek His face continually."

   PS 34:10 –"Even strong young lions sometimes go hungry, but those who trust in (seek) the Lord will never lack any good thing."

   Matt. 6:33 –"But seek ye first His kingdom and His righteousness and all these things shall be added unto you."

_____

_____

_____

_____

_____

DAY 78

Nothing compares to the promises I have in You. Your word defines life. Your Word is life. It is living and became flesh and dwelt among men. It is a light in the darkness for mankind to follow. Without that light we are hopelessly lost in an over-whelming world of powers and principalities. Without you Lord, there is no help. God, you give me blessings overflowing in abundance. I go from day to day being blessed and protected by your love, your word. I can't even imagine the evil that is aimed at me each day that you turn back, without me ever knowing about it.

One does not have to search for those things that God has done for them, if they are walking in His word. We cannot take for granted the joy, peace and love we have in life. Those things are not there because we are wise. They are in place because of the promises you have given to us. Money, fame or popularity cannot buy the satisfaction that you provide. In you, circumstance doesn't matter. Nothing can cut us off from the love You have and want to give. We are bought and paid for! Christ did it! Thank you Jesus.

Bible reference; Notes

1. Living;

     PS 27:13 –"Yet I am confident that I will see the Lord's goodness while I am here in the land of the living."

     Mark 12:26-27 –Jesus speaking –"…God said to Moses 'I am the God of Abraham and the God of Jacob.' So He is the God of the living, not the dead."

     John 6:57 – Jesus speaking –"I live by the power of the living Father who sent me…those who partake of me will live because of me."

2. Word;

     PS 33:4 –"For the word of the Lord holds true and everything He does is worthy of our trust."

     PS 119:11 –"I have hidden your word in my heart that I might not sin against you."

     Luke 4:4 – Jesus speaking –"It is written; man shall not live by bread alone, but by every word of God."

3. Evil;

     PS 23:4 –"Even when I walk through the dark valley of death I will not be afraid (will fear no evil) for you are close beside me…"

     Matt. 6:22-23 – Jesus speaking –"Your eye is a lamp for your body. A pure eye lets sunshine into your soul. But an evil eye shuts out the light and plunges you into darkness…"

     John 3:20 – Jesus speaking –"For everyone who does evil hates the light and does not come to the light, lest his (evil) deeds should be exposed."

_____

_____

_____

_____

DAY 79

This day O Lord is a day you have made. I want to walk fully in your way. I want to remain under the cover of your wing. Every moment I have, every moment I am, I want it to be guided by your Holy Spirit. There is not a breath I take, not a heartbeat I have that I don't want covered by your love and protection. When I write these entries I always wonder, did I remain under the shadow of the Almighty as much as I could have? This is where my thanksgiving comes from. It is for Your goodness of course, but it is for those moments I truly walked in Your paths. I thank You. You are my joy and my blessings.

The sadness or regret comes when I find I have been distracted and took my eyes off of you or when my iniquities overshadowed your presence in that moment of my day. I live for the time when we will all be able to see you face to face and bask continually in your presence, knowing your fullness in complete fellowship with You. I am joyful now for your presence in my life. I can't imagine the limitless joy that will be mine when I am complete in You!

Bible reference; Notes

1. Walk;

    Deu. 5:33 –"You shall walk in the way which the Lord your God has commanded you that you may live and that it may be well with you, and that you may prolong your days…"

    PS 119:1 –"How blessed are they whose way is blameless who walk in the law of the Lord."

    John 8:12 – Jesus speaking –"I am the light of the world; he who follows me shall not walk in the darkness but shall have the light of life."

2. Covered;

    PS 32:1 –"Oh what joy for those whose rebellion is forgiven, whose sin is (covered) put out of sight."

    Luke 12:2 – Jesus' words –"For there is nothing covered up that will not be revealed and hidden that will not be known."

    Rom. 4:7 –"Blessed are those whose lawless deeds have been forgiven and whose sins have been covered."

3. Guide;

    PS 31:3 –"For (you) are my rock and fortress. For (Your) names sake (You) will lead me and guide me."

    Luke 1:78-79 –"Because of God's tender mercy, the light from Heaven is about to break upon us, to give light to those who sit in darkness and in the shadow of death and to guide us to the path of peace."

    John 16:13 – Jesus' words –"When the Spirit of Truth comes, He will guide you into all truth…"

_____

_____

_____

_____

"Nothing compares to the promise I have in you. My Jesus, my savior." Lord, I thank you for the blessings I received from you even before I was born. I gave no thought or made no preparation for my inheritance, my place of origin, my language or my parents. Yet, God, You provided all of these things for me, even before my conception!

Who among us can prepare the time, place, situation, language or parents we receive at birth? None, absolutely none. It was God who did all those things in order to bless us. He has planned for us a future and health, not defeat and sickness. When we begin to believe the lies of the evil one and feel like we earned or deserve these things, then we have taken on a stronghold that blinds us to the truth.

God's word is truth. All else will change, all else will vanish, only His word will remain. God, I thank you that the only righteousness I have is in you. You so completely cover me with the Blood of Christ that you see only His righteousness when you consider me. With it I have the right to boldly come into your very presence.

Bible reference; Notes

1. Savior;

    Isa. 19:20 –"…When the people cry to the Lord for help against those who oppress them, He will send them a savior who will rescue them."

    2 Tim. 1:10 –"And now He (God) has made all of this plain to us by the coming of Christ Jesus, our Savior, who broke the power (of sin) and showed us the way to everlasting life…"

    1 John 4:14 –"Furthermore, we have seen with our own eyes and now testify that the Father sent His Son to be the Savior of the world."

2. Jesus;

    Matt. 1:21&25 –"And she will have a son and you are to name Him Jesus, for He will save His people from their sins…but she remained a virgin until her son was born and Joseph named Him Jesus."

    Matt. 4:17 –"From then on Jesus began to preach (His words)…'turn from your sins and turn to God because the Kingdom of Heaven is near.'"

    John 20:19-21 –"Suddenly Jesus was standing there among them…They were filled with joy when they saw their Lord. He said –'Peace be with you, as the Father has sent me so send I you…Receive the Holy Spirit…'"

3. Proof;

    PS 47:3 –"He subdues the nations before us, putting our enemies beneath our feet."

    PS 139:16 –"You saw me before I was born. Every day of my life was recorded in your book; every moment was laid out before a single day had passed."

Heb. 4:16 –"So let us come boldly to the throne of our gracious God. There we will receive His mercy and we will find grace to help us when we need it."

_____

_____

_____

_____

_____

_____

DAY 81

Dear Lord, aging is a scary process. Daily I awake to new pain. I wake up during the night with pain, my body hurts, and its capacity is diminished. My eyes grow dull, my hearing escapes me. Yet, to my eyes, things still appear to me as they did in the strength of my youth. I really don't understand the process; it is all so new to me. I've never been here before and have to learn new things daily. In all this I can still rejoice and be glad in you. You answer all prayer. All my requests to fix this or remove that will surely be answered. Those things in my physical body will be fixed either here or in the hereafter, I have no doubt.

These infirmities are all signs that I am being prepared to change, to go through metamorphosis, as it were, for a new bodily form. It will be one that is meant to be with the Father, directly in His presence without blemish or fault. I will be like the eternal beings, but better. My form will be perfect, no sagging, and no limited or painful movements. For this, my God, I am grateful. I thank you now for the beauty I am about to behold!

Bible reference; Notes

1. Old;

    <u>PS 37:25&27</u> –"Once I was young and now I am old. Yet I have never seen the godly forsaken nor seen their children begging for bread…Turn from evil and do good and you will live in the land forever…"

    <u>PS 71:9&14</u> –"And now in my old age, don't set me aside. Don't abandon me when my strength is failing…I will keep on hoping for you to help me; I will praise you (God) more and more."

    <u>Acts 2:17</u> –"In the last days, God said, I will pour out My Spirit upon all people. Your sons and daughters will prophecy; your young men will see visions and your old men will dream dreams."

2. Infirmities;

    <u>Matt. 8:17</u> –"This fulfilled the word of the Lord through Isaiah who said, 'He took our sickness (infirmities) and removed our disease.' "

    <u>Rom. 8:26</u> –"And the Holy Spirit helps us in our distress (infirmities), for we don't even know what we should pray for nor how we should pray. But the Holy Spirit prays for us with groaning that cannot be expressed in words."

    <u>Rom 15:1</u> –"Now we who are strong ought to bear the weakness (infirmities) of those without strength (old) and not just to please ourselves."

3. New;

    <u>Isa. 65:17</u> –"Look, I am creating new heavens and a new earth – so wonderful that no one will even think about the old ones anymore."

    <u>2 Cor. 5:17</u> –"What this means is that those who become Christians become new persons. They are not the same anymore for the old life is gone, a new life has begun."

<u>Eph. 4:24</u> –"You must display a new nature because you are a new person, created in God's likeness, righteous, holy and true."

_____

_____

_____

_____

_____

_____

DAY 82

God, you overcame all obstacles in my life. Your promises are so fresh and true it is just as if they were given today instead of over two-thousand years ago. The Gospel does not get stale. It is alive, your word is living. It came to us through the Holy Spirit. It is a philosophy, the only true philosophy, for life. Without your word we would be stuck following some man-made set of rules that serve to chain the soul and capture the spirit. Thank you, Father that you have set us free, free from the law of sin and death. Thank you God that we are independent agents, free to choose obedience to your word or obedience to the law. (I choose Your Word.)

When we move out from under your word we become a slave to the law, which was given only to condemn. I can see the attempt now, in this country by our President, to diminish the importance of Your Word and increase the effect of the law of man. This nation is rapidly becoming a third-rate power because we, as a nation, are moving out from under Your Word Lord, to the specter of Secular Humanism and the "vainly imagined" intelligence of the law of man. Though we are in chains, our Spirits are free and You have made us that way. Praise Your Holy Name!

Bible reference; Notes

1. Overcomes;

    1 John 5:4 –"For every Child of God defeats (overcomes) this evil world by trusting Christ to give the victory."

    1 John 5:5 –"And the ones who win this battle against the world (overcomes the world) are the ones who believe that Jesus is the Son of God."

    Rev. 2:7&11 – Jesus' words –"Anyone who is willing to hear should listen to the Spirit and understand… Everyone who is victorious (overcomes) will eat from the Tree of Life in the Paradise of God…will not be hurt by the second death."

2. Promise;

    Acts 2:38-39 –"…Each of you must turn from your sins and turn to God and be baptized in the name of Jesus Christ for the forgiveness of your sins. This promise is to you and your children…"

    Rom. 4:13 –"It is clear then, that God's promise to give the whole world to Abraham and his descendants (believers) was not based on obedience to God's law, but on the new relationship with God that comes by faith."

    Rom. 4:16 –"So that is why faith is the key! God's promise is given to us as a free gift and we are certain to receive it…if we have faith…"

3. Gospel;

    Matt. 24:14 – Jesus' words –"And the Good News (Gospel) about the Kingdom will be preached throughout the whole world, so that all nations will hear it, and then, finally, the end will come."

<u>Mark 16:15</u> – Jesus' words –"Go into all the world and preach the Good News (Gospel) to everyone everywhere."

<u>Gal. 1:8</u> – "Let God's curse fall on anyone, including myself, who preaches any other message (Gospel) than the one we told you about. Even if an angel comes from Heaven and preaches any other message (Gospel) let him forever be cursed."

_____

_____

_____

_____

_____

_____

DAY 83

God, time is nothing to you. Your view of our life gives you a certainty of our outcome. But, viewed through my eyes it is a daily struggle with seemingly endless chances to lose focus and stray from your way. It is so hard for me to "stay on task", as it were, to walk in complete fellowship with you. In my daily prayer life I, sometimes, am keenly aware of your presence. At other times you seem so far away. However, I do know that during those "dry" times in my spirit it is not you who have moved away, it is I. I have moved away from you. Your word says you will never leave nor forsake me. Thank you, Lord that my salvation does not depend upon me. I always want you to hold me, I know you will never fail me and that is a great source of joy!

I base my belief upon your word, upon your promises. I am saved, safe and secure! You are there and you know me, you know what I have done, what I am doing and what I shall do. There is such security in your word. There is life in Your Word. God I desire to always walk in your light. Please continue to keep me until the day of your glorious appearing!

Bible reference; Notes

1. Year;

   PS 90:4 –"For you (Lord) a thousand years are as yesterday. They are like a few hours."

   2 Peter 3:8-9 –"But you must not forget dear friends, that a day is like a thousand years to the Lord, and a thousand years is like a day. The Lord isn't really being slow about His promise to return as some people think."

   Rev. 20:6 –"Blessed and holy are those who share in the first resurrection. For then the second death has no power but they will be priests of God and of Christ and will reign with him a thousand years."

2. Daily;

   PS 68:19 –"Praise the Lord; praise God our Savior! For each day (daily) he carries us in his arms.

   Luke 9:23 –Jesus' words –"If any of you want to be my follower, you must put aside your selfish ambition, shoulder your cross daily and follow me."

   Heb. 3:13 –"You must warn each other every day (daily), as long as it is called 'today', so that none of you will be deceived by sin and hardened against God."

3. Glorious;

   1 Chron. 29:13 –"O our God, we thank you and praise your glorious name."

   PS 66:2 –"Sing about the glory of His name! Tell the world how glorious He is."

   2 Cor. 4:4 –"Satan, the god of this evil world, has blinded the minds of those who don't believe, so they are unable to see the glorious light of the Good News that is shining upon them…"

_____

_____

_____

_____

_____

DAY 84

Physical health is a blessing that comes from our Lord. It is His desire that we are healthy and function well. God, you have blessed me with health and abundance, and I praise your name for it! Along with a healthy body Lord, you have given common sense. Our spiritual and physical body respond to the principles you have set in place. It is through you that we can refrain from over indulgence or under indulgence in certain aspects of life, such as eating, diet and exercise. I know I am not where I should be and pray for a desire to subdue the natural desires of my body which will lead to over indulgence. Thank you God for a sound mind. Thank you for the mind of Christ and the will of God which frees me from slavery to sin.

I see how I naturally desire to follow my own cravings. I thank you for the will and knowledge not to completely give in to the things of this world. You give me comfort, Lord, in knowing that I am not in this battle alone. Your strength and righteousness sustain me. How fearful it would be not having the Holy Spirit to sustain me!

Bible reference; Notes

1. Abundance;

    Matt. 13:12 – Jesus' words –"To those who are open to my teaching, more understanding will be given and they will have an abundance of knowledge."

    Matt. 25:29 – Jesus' words –"To those who use well what they are given, even more will be given, and they will have an abundance."

    Luke 12:15 – Jesus' words –"Then He said, 'Beware, don't be greedy for what you don't have. Real life is not measured by how much we own'" (our abundance).

2. Subdue;

    Micah 7:19 – Turn to God and –"once again you (God) will have compassion on us. You will trample (subdue) our sins under your feet and throw them into the depths of the ocean."

    Phil. 3:21 –"He will take these weak mortal bodies of ours and change them into glorious bodies like His own, using the same mighty power that He will use to conquer (subdue) everything everywhere."

    1 Cor. 15:28 –"Then when He has conquered (subdued) all things, the Son will present Himself to God, so that God who gave His son authority over all things, will be utterly supreme over everything everywhere."

3. Mind;

    Isa. 26:3 –"You will keep in perfect peace all who trust in you, whose thoughts (mind) are fixed on you."

    Rom. 12:2 –"Don't copy the customs and behaviors of this world, but let God transform you into a new person by changing the way you think (your mind). Then you will know what God wants you to do…"

<u>Phil. 2:5-6</u> – "Have this attitude (mind) in yourselves which was also in Christ Jesus, who, although He existed in the form of God did not regard equality with God a thing to be grasped."

_____

_____

_____

_____

_____

_____

DAY 85

Lord, you watch over me even when I am not aware. The new covenant you have made with me does not stop nor does it diminish. You are consistent and steady, never varying, never even hesitating. You are my Rock and my Fortress. I, on the other hand, change and wobble in my walk with you. From the moment I open my eyes in the morning I walk in and out of your will like a drunken sailor, trying to maintain a steady gait down the sidewalk. Thank You, Jesus, for your mercy, grace and forgiveness. I would be completely lost without you. Life would be completely meaningless and without purpose. But because You are there, because You are constant, loyal and true I have a purpose, a meaning and a future. That future includes the blessings of my children.

You, O Lord, have blessed us with two wonderful, whole, precious children. In them you will continue your blessings upon my life. Thank you, Father. Your ways are so much higher than my ways. I can never be good enough to deserve or earn the love you have poured out for me. You loved us before we were born. You called us by name! Bless Your Holy Name.

Bible reference; Notes

1. Thoughts;

    PS 40:5 –"O Lord my God, you have done so many miracles for us. Your plans (thoughts) for us are too numerous to list. If I tried to recite all your wonderful deeds I would never come to the end of them."

    PS 139:17 –"How precious are your thoughts about me O God! They are innumerable."

    Jer. 29:11 –"For I know the plans (thoughts) I have for you," says the Lord. "They are plans (thoughts) for good and not for disaster, to give you a future and a hope."

2. Children;

    PS 127:3 –"Children are a gift from the Lord; they are a reward from Him."

    Prov. 13:24 –"If you refuse to discipline your children, it proves you don't love them; if you love your children you will be prompt to discipline them."

    Gal. 3:25-26 –"But now that (your) faith in Christ has come, we no longer need the law as our guardian. So you (we) are all children of God through (our) faith in Christ Jesus."

3. Blessed;

    Deu. 30:16 –"…Love the Lord your God and keep His commandments…if you do this you will live and become a great nation and the Lord your God will bless you…"

    PS 112:1-2 –"…How blessed is the man who fears the Lord, who greatly delights in His commandments, His descendants shall be mighty on the earth. The generation of the upright will be blessed."

2 Cor. 1:3 –"All praise (blessings) to the God and Father of our Lord Jesus Christ. He is the source of every mercy (blessing) and the God who comforts us."

_____

_____

_____

_____

_____

_____

DAY 86

To God, not to us, be the glory. It is He who has made us. We are the sheep of His pasture; therefore enter into His gates with praise, into His presence with thanksgiving. God is always diligent, always watchful. He never sleeps. We can rest, sleep and His love does not leave us. He is an ever present source of help.

The political times in this country now are very uncertain. The present administration is changing this society to a socialistic society; we are turning away from the precepts of the Founding Fathers and the Law of the Land which is the U.S. Constitution. The administration has already violated it in many different ways and there are many lawsuits against some of the things it has done.

God is our source of comfort in every situation. No matter what happens on this earth, in this country, God is in control. Our current situation is not God's fault. Ancient Israel got their king even though God warned them against having an earthly king. This nation has turned into a secular humanistic society of people who want their way, not Gods. He allows this, because we are a people of free will. God so loved the world that He gave His Son. It is our choice to choose Him or not. Thank you Lord for the choice to come to You!

Bible reference; Notes

1. Know;

    <u>PS 100:3</u> –"Know that the Lord Himself is God. It is He who has made us and not we ourselves. We are His people and the sheep of His pasture."

    <u>2 Tim. 1:12</u> –"…for I know whom I have believed an am persuaded that He is able to keep that which I have committed unto Him against that day."

    <u>1 John 2:5-6</u> –"But those who obey God's word really do love Him. That is the way to know whether or not we live in Him. Those who say they live in God should live their lives as Christ did."

2. Glory;

    <u>1 Chron. 16:25&27</u> –"Great is the Lord. He is most worthy of praise! Honor and majesty (Glory) surround Him; strength and beauty are in His dwelling."

    <u>PS 62:7</u> –"My salvation and my honor (Glory) came from God alone. He is my refuge, a Rock where no enemy can reach me."

    <u>Luke 21:27</u> – Jesus' words –"Then everyone will see the Son of Man arrive on the clouds with power and great glory!"

3. People;

    <u>Deu.7:6</u> –"For you are a holy people, who belong to the Lord your God. Of all the people on earth, the Lord your God has chosen you to be His own special treasure."

    <u>2 Chron. 7:14</u> –"Then if my people who are called by my name will humble themselves and pray and seek my face and turn from their wicked ways, I will hear their prayer from heaven, forgive their sins and heal their land."

2 Cor.6:16 –"…For we are the temple of the living God. As God said, 'I will live in them and walk among them. I will be their God and they shall be my people'".

_____

_____

_____

_____

_____

_____

DAY 87

Today, Wednesday, is a "pick me up" night. We go to meet with our church family, fellow believers who love the Lord. Everyone has a testimony. Underneath the wrappings, all of us testify of the power of Christ in our lives. All tell of the blessings and changes God has brought into our lives. It is wonderful hearing about His work in other people. It makes a person realize that the wrapping is not important. It makes one realize that God works in believers the same way but not necessarily in the same circumstances. By listening to these testimonies of others, one feels that that individual has confirmed something in their life that God has provided.

It is wonderful to be affirmed because of the testimony of others. I believe this is what God created the church for. When you are in belief of God alone, without the benefit of hearing others, you grow "lumpy or one sided" and begin to look upon God's involvement with you in a peculiar way. Sometimes this causes the building up of strongholds that interfere with the work of the Holy Spirit in your life. I praise God for His wisdom in telling us not to forbid ourselves fellowship with like believers. Truly it is a blessing to be a part of the family of God.

Bible reference; Notes

1. Fellowship;

    1 John 1:3 –"We are telling you about what we ourselves have actually seen and heard, so that you may have fellowship with us. And our fellowship is with the Father and His Son Jesus Christ."

    1 John 1:7 –"…if we are living in the light of God's presence, just as Christ is, then we have fellowship with each other and the blood of Jesus, His Son, cleanses us from every sin."

    1 Cor. 1:9 –"God will surely do all this for you, for He always does just what He says, and He is the one who invited you into this wonderful fellowship with His Son Jesus Christ our Lord."

2. Testimony;

    PS 19:7 –"The law of the Lord is perfect, restoring the soul; the testimony of the Lord is sure, making wise the simple."

    John 3:33 –"Those who believe Him (receive His testimony) discover that God is true."

    2 Tim. 1:8-9 –"Therefore do not be ashamed of the testimony of our Lord…who has called us with an holy calling, not according to our works, but according to His own purpose…"

3. Hearing;

    Matt. 7:24 – Jesus' words –"Anyone who listens to (hears) my teaching and obeys me is wise, like a man who builds his house on a solid rock."

    Luke 6:49 –Jesus' words –"But anyone who listens (hears) and doesn't obey is like a person who builds his house without a foundation."

Rom. 10:17 –"So, faith comes from hearing, and hearing by the Word of Christ." (The Good News of Christ.)

_____

_____

_____

_____

_____

_____

DAY 88

Great sadness fills my heart when I see the condition of the family life of some of the children who are assigned to the facility where I work. I only get a snap shot view of their lives as I interact daily with them in the classroom situation. I know they have been assigned to residential care for the things they have done. I just can't help but think that with a more God centered environment at home they wouldn't be sentenced to this facility. I see their young faces lined with anger, hurt, betrayal and disappointment. When they leave the facility I have no idea what happens to them. The bright part of it all is that I know that there is a God, my God, who deeply cares for and loves them. I pray that they will have their eyes opened and that they will invite Christ into their heart to be master of their lives.

That is my joy. I know that if God loved me so much as to give His only begotten Son, He loves them just as much. Thank you, Lord, for the brightness and hope you provide in our lives. Thank you for the strength that is in your love for us. Thank you for Jesus our Savior!

Bible reference; Notes

1. Family;

    Deu. 29:18 –"The Lord made this (His) covenant with you so that no man, woman, family or tribe would turn away from the Lord our God…"

    Acts 16:30-34 – The jailer –"Sirs, what must I do to be saved? They replied, 'Believe on the Lord Jesus and you will be saved, along with your entire household (family).' He and his (family) rejoiced because they all believed in God."

    Eph. 3:14-15 –"For this reason I bow my knees before the Father, from whom every family in heaven and on earth derives its name."

2. Anger;

    PS 37:8 –"Stop your anger! Turn from your rage. Do not envy others; it only leads to harm."

    Prov. 16:32 –"He who is slow to anger is better than the mighty and he who rules his spirit (self-control) than he who captures a city."

    Eph. 4:31-32 –"Get rid of bitterness, rage, anger, harsh words and slander as well as all types of malicious behavior. Instead be kind…tenderhearted, just as…Christ has forgiven you."

3. Believe;

    John 1:12 –"But to all who believe in Him and accepted Him, He gave the right to become children of God. They are reborn!"

    John 8:24 – Jesus' words –"That is why I say you will die in your sins; For unless you believe I am who I say I am, you will die in your sins."

    1 Thes. 4:14 –"For since we believe that Jesus died and was raised to life again, we also believe that when Jesus comes, God will bring back with Jesus all the Christians who have died."

_____

_____

_____

_____

_____

_____

DAY 89

Lord, when I consider the works of your hands, the sun, the moon, the stars, the birds of the air, the beast of the fields, the fish in the sea and whatsoever passes through the paths of the sea, what is man (Me) that you are mindful of me? Of all the magnificent things you have made, how could you consider me such that you sent your only begotten Son to suffer and die for my sins? You, who spoke the worlds into existence, take note of me! You have provided me with a life of abundance. You have provided me with a steady family, a wonderful mate, two great children and you also provide me with consistent daily care and health.

What is not to like about being a child of God? How can people choose not to believe, choose not to obey? Why is there an argument about obedience to you? O' Lord my God, how excellent is your name in all the earth! Out of the mouths of babes and weaklings have you ordained strength. The weak have been made strong, the poor have been made rich. You and You alone are God. It is you who have made us, and not we ourselves. Therefore I enter into your presence with praise!

Bible reference; Notes

1. Works;

    <u>Deu. 3:24</u> –"O sovereign Lord, I am your servant. You have only begun to show me your greatness and power. Is there any God in heaven or on earth who can perform such great deeds (works) as yours?

    <u>PS 78:4</u> –"We will not hide these truths from our children, but will tell (them) about the glorious deeds of the Lord. We will tell of His power and the mighty deeds (works) He did."

    <u>John 10:38</u> – Jesus' words –"But if I do this work, believe in what I have done, even if you don't believe me. Then you will realize that the Father is in me and I am in the Father."

2. Son;

    <u>Matt. 1:21</u> –"And she will have a son and you are to name Him Jesus, for He will save His people from their sins."

    <u>Mark 2:10</u> – Jesus' words –"I will prove that I, the Son of Man, have the authority on earth to forgive sins. Then Jesus…said, 'Stand up, take up your mat and go on home, because you are healed."

    <u>Acts 9:20</u> – Paul's eyes were healed –"And immediately he began preaching about Jesus in the synagogues saying, 'He indeed is the Son of God.'"

3. Abundantly;

    <u>John 10:9-10</u> – Jesus' words –"Yes, I am the gate. Those who come in through me will be saved…My purpose is to give life in all its fullness (abundantly)."

    <u>Eph. 3:20</u> –"Now glory be to God! By His mighty power at work within us, he is able to accomplish infinitely (abundantly) more than we would ever do or ask or hope."

2 Peter 1:11 –"And God will open wide (abundantly) the gates of heaven for you to enter into the eternal Kingdom of our Lord and Savior Jesus Christ."

_____

_____

_____

_____

_____

_____

DAY 90

Jesus, you are savior of my soul. From day to day I live and function in the physical world. I am involved in the problems of the day. As each day passes I get further away from Sunday where I rub elbows with worshiping folks. My spiritual fire seems to dull somewhat. Wednesday comes and I get charged up again and then have to struggle through until Sunday. The beauty of it is that God doesn't change. He is the same yesterday, today and tomorrow. I struggle for the same type of consistency and I can't achieve it. I can't live daily on a level plain with my God. However, my ups and downs don't deter Him from loving me.

That's what I'm talking about! That's my God, Jesus. He had all this stuff figured out way before He created the heavens and the earth. Even then He knew who would and who wouldn't respond to His call. I am so thankful He did it all. I am complete only in Him. To worry about how to escape the fate of all mortal men (death) is more than a person can bear. To realize that the plan has been prearranged is a glorious thing! Jesus paid it all. I have a prepaid first class ticket to my final destination! Praise the Lord!

Bible reference; Notes

1. Savior;

   2 Sam. 22:2-3 –"The Lord is my rock, my fortress and my savior. My God is my rock, in whom I find protection. He is my shield, the strength of my salvation, and my stronghold, my high tower, my savior, the one who saves me from violence."

   Luke 1:47 –"My soul exalts the Lord and my spirit has rejoiced in God my savior."

   1 John 4:14 –"Furthermore, we have seen with our own eyes and now testify that the Father sent his Son to be the Savior of the world."

2. Remain;

   PS 102:26 –"Even they (Earth and Heavens) will perish, but you remain forever. They will wear out… and will fade away, but you are always the same; your years never end."

   PS 110:4 – Speaking of Jesus –"The Lord has taken an oath and will not break His vow, 'You are a priest forever in the line of Melchizedek.'"

   Heb. 7:24 –"But Jesus remains a priest forever, His priesthood will never end." (Remains)

3. Victory;

   1 Chron. 29:11 –"Yours O Lord is the greatness, the power, the glory, the victory and the majesty. Everything in Heaven and on earth is yours."

   Isa. 25:8 –"He will swallow up death in victory; and the Lord God will wipe away tears from all faces… for the Lord has spoken it."

   1 Cor. 15:54-55 –"When this happens – when our perishable earthly bodies have been transformed into heavenly bodies that will never die…Death is swallowed up in victory. O death, where is your victory? O death, where is your sting?"

Kenneth L. Canion

_____

_____

_____

_____

_____

_____

POSTSCRIPT

"A Walk in Faith" was written as the result of a year-long assignment of recording daily thoughts in the involvement of my life in God. I feel that the accompanying scripture verses point out that every thought, every breath, every moment in the life of mankind can be related to an act or a plan that God has already provided for us.

His presence in this world and our lives completely covers every possible situation or circumstance that one can come upon. My intent is to provide scripture references for this three month portion of the 365 day journal, and publish it as a testimony that there is nothing in life that is not covered by God's magnificent plan and foreknowledge while here on earth.

For the sake of clarity, I have used three versions of the Bible. Versions of the Bible used for quotes include; Life Application Study Bible – New Living Translation, Tyndale; The New Open Bible – New American Standard, Nelson; The New Scofield Reference Bible – Authorized KJV, Oxford University Press.

To God be the glory and the power and the honor for ever and ever, Amen.

Author/Biography

Kenneth L. Canion was born prior to the end of WW II (1944), a member of the little known "Builder Generation." His father retired from the military, he and his twin sisters spent their public school years in a small town working in the family owned "mom and pop" grocery store.

Kenneth graduated from Texas A&M with a B.S. and, after his time in the USAF as a B-52 Navigator (Viet Nam era) earned a Masters of Education in Curriculum and Instruction.

Kenneth has also earned a Certificate of Ordination and license as a minister of the Gospel of Jesus Christ from Bay City Living Word World Outreach Center, Incorporated, Brazoria, Texas. In addition, he has completed requirements for a PhD in Christian Counseling from World Outreach International Bible College.